THE
FINAL
BOUNDARY

For
Humankind

A
MATTER
OF
SURVIVAL!

ENTERING THOUGHTS

In life's ebb and flow, there are little waves and big ones, joys, and troubles. The way we sail these not only affects our own lives, but everyone-indeed the whole progression of humankind because every ripple combines lending force to the swell. So, the thoughtful must ask piercing questions.

Are we living our lives with the waves simply taking us along to final storm, or have we conquered them sailing controlled under our own power, recognizing destiny-to a safe harbor?

Are the rising waves shattering on the rocky shore of the damned or is our course one forever rising magnificently-taking us into a bright securing future?

Will the inevitable swelling, the "Final Declaration of Humanity" be a war of bombs, or of words, will it become a tragic crash born in its earliest misdirected ripples, or the powerful welling of predestined-united seas carrying all to a far distant but beautiful eternity?

Quoted from "Light Found', ISBN: 978-0-615-47403-8 (2011) by the author of this book, D.M.Yourtee.

"THE FINAL BOUNDARY "
by D.M. Yourtee
Copywrite, 2024 ©

This book traces its origin to humanitarian research by the author in Africa and the teaching there by an extraordinary visionary, African woman. That encounter is recorded in the book "The Final Human, A Vistavien Proposal" ISBN: 097811454X. That book is out of print but may be obtained through the publisher listed below.

This Work is
Published by Minds-Eye Manuscripts, LLC
Grand Junction, CO 81505
Minds-Eye@bresnan.net

FORWARD

The author's mother used to say "Son, you act like you are from Mars"! Well, I am sure I was a bit of a problem as a teenager. Even so, he admits to being not Martian, but a Homo sapiens, or a human, along with the rest of you able to read this.

Where is it all going… being human? Certainly, at least, we hope there is a Boundary—where we Homo sapiens (the species, in heaven or not) cross to be their very best—to last even beyond that promised ending, i.e. the Omega Point. Will we not survive to be up-step or to coin a logical scientific notation "Homo Vistavien"[1]?

We rarely think about this, we just exist as we are assuming this is it, as such. But it is important, if we want our future children to go on, to enjoy being the masters of the stars, which I argue we might deserve.

Where are we and on present behavior where are we likely to go? Here following fellow Sapiens is your story and your potential onward to be "Vistaviens".

---

[1] Blame this author for this, proposed it in the books, The "Final Human" 9781145-4-X & "The Future Navigator" ISBN: 978-0-692-40588-8.

DEDICATION

This work is dedicated to the Children of this World present and future and is presented in the sincerest hope that theirs' will become a better and more secure world.

CHAPTER LOCATIONS

This document is formed from worthy quotes using an adaptation of the APA method of citation. Information to be quoted is identified with a lead reference number in the text and then the following information is surrounded by paragraph quotation marks. Where the cited article contains information by other authors those are credited by name. Reference to the lead article for reader follow up is given in "Acknowledgements". Where you see text in italics-those are editorial comments by this author, providing his emphasis.

CHAPTER 1: BOUNDARIES

The Matter of an Edge

Well to begin, most of us recognize there are many, many boundaries: The boundary between slow and fast, right and wrong, between good and evil, between peace and war, and so sadly between faith and killing.

Even so, we fail to face the fact that no boundary-given our remarkable development, is more important than the beginning and transition to the ending (or forever continuing) of human life.

Yes, boundaries! But of course, every boundary has edges. There is the edge just crossed, the in-between and the edge over the "Final Boundary" from which the commitment is made and there is no returning.

We try to make the crossing-the evaluation between one beginning side and the other ending side for almost all the boundaries, but we ignore that "Final One"!

This essay addresses that: "Facing Our Final Boundary".

What is that boundary… It can be seen through eyes postulating something called the "OMEGA POINT." *For a needed definition we shall call the onset to that point, a delineated, i.e. specified region the "EDGE."*

The Omega Point is a spiritual belief that everything in the universe is fated to spiral towards a final point of divine unification. Herein we will call that "point" the "Terminus", in effect the finality of human kind per se.

1._ "The term was coined by the French Jesuit Catholic priest Pierre Teilhard de Chardin (1881-1955). This priest, in proposing, not a proposal favored by the church argued that the Omega Point resembles the Christian Logos, namely Christ, who draws all things into himself, who in the words of the Nicene Creed, is 'God from God', 'Light from Light', 'True God from true God', and through Him all things were made. In the Book of Revelation, Christ describes Himself thrice as the Alpha and the Omega, the beginning and the end."

2._ The idea of the Omega Point is developed in later writings, such as those of John David Garcia (1971), Paolo Soleri (1981), Frank Tipler (1994), and David Deutsch (1997). Here following is an overview of the precepts, arguments in this cosmology. The theory was proposed in 1947."

"Historical Development: Teilhard de Chardin was a paleontologist and Roman Catholic priest in the Jesuit order. In France in the 1920s, he began incorporating his theories of the universe into lectures that placed Catholicism and evolution in the same conversation."

"Because of these lectures, he was suspected by the Holy Office of denying the doctrine of original sin. This caused Teilhard to be exiled to China and banned from publication by Church authorities. It was not until one year after his death, in 1955, that his writings were published for the world to read. His book 'The Phenomenon of Man' has been dissected by astrophysicists and cosmologists to be a theological or philosophical theory that cannot be scientifically proven. However, as one who dared to propose an ending of us, it deserves description. Teilhard, who was not a cosmologist, opens his books with the statement: if this book is to be properly understood, it must be read not as a work on metaphysics, still less than a sort of theological essay, but purely and a simply as a scientific treatise."

"Theological Controversy: It is noteworthy that Pierre Teilhard de Chardin's life (1881-1955) falls directly in between the First Vatican Council (1869) and the Second Vatican Council (1965), a time period where increasing global acceptance of evolution was forming a disconnect between modern humanity and the Roman Catholic Church. And, His time came shortly after Charles Darwin's 1859 book, 'On the Origin of Species'. A time when the intersection between the claims of scientific theories and the claims of traditional theological teachings became an enormous focus of the Vatican's agenda."

"Evolution: Evolution does not end with mankind: Earth's biosphere evolved before humans existed. Teilhard describes evolution as earth's 'hominization' in which one-cell organisms develop into metazoans, or animals, but some members of this classification develop organisms with complex nervous systems. This group has the capability to acquire intelligence. When Homo sapiens inhabited Earth through evolution, a 'Noosphere', the cognitive layer of existence, was created. As evolution continues, the noosphere gains coherence. Teilhard refers to this process as 'planarization'. Eventually, the noosphere gains total dominance over the biosphere and reaches a point of complete independence from tangential energy forming a metaphysical being, that Teilhard coined as the Omega Point."

"Energy: Energy exists in two basic modes as follows. Tangential Energy is energy that can be measured by physics. Radial Energy is spiritual energy which accumulates into a higher state as time progresses Teilhard defines Radial Energy as becoming more concentrated and available as it is a critical element in man's evolution. The theory applies to all forms of matter, concluding that everything with existence has some sort of life. In regard to Teilhard's, 'The Phenomenon of Man', Peter Medawar wrote, "Teilhard's radial, spiritual, or psychic energy may be equated to information or information content, in the sense that has been made reasonably precise by communication engineers."

"Formal properties: Teilhard's theory is maintained by four formal properties as follows:
Humans will escape the heat death of the universe. Scientifically, this means that intelligence cannot survive! He theorizes that since radial energy is non-compliant with entropy, it escapes the collapses of forces at the world's end."

"The Omega Point does not exist within the timeline of the universe, it occurs at the exact edge of the end of time. From that point, all sequence of existence is sucked into its being."

"The Omega Point can be understood as a volume shaped as a cone in which each section taken from the base to its summit decreases until it diminishes into a final point."

"The volume described in the Third Property must be understood as an entity with finite boundaries. Teilhard explains: ...what would have become of humanity, if, by some remote chance, it had been free to spread indefinitely on an unlimited surface, which is to say left only to the devices of its internal affinities? Something unimaginable, perhaps even nothing at all when we think of the extreme important of the role played in its development by the forces of compression."

"Forces of Compression: Teilhard calls the contributing universal energy that generates the Omega Point 'forces of compression'. Unlike the scientific definition, which incorporates gravity and mass, Teilhard's forces of compression sources from communication and contact between human beings. This value is limitless and directly correlated with entropy. It suggests that as humans continue to interact, consciousness evolves and grows."

"For the theory to occur, humans must also be bound to the finite earth. Creation of this boundary forces the world's convergence upon itself which he theorizes to result in time ending in communion with the Omega Point-God."

This portion of Teilhard's thinking shows his lack of expectation for humans to engage in space travel and transcend past the borders of the planet at a place chosen in the cosmos's forever. [1] And it relays the lack of expectation that the human mind cannot preserve itself, maintain its mental freedom and intelligence, and exist within the ever existing Mobius Cosmos.

---

[1] The "Forever Cosmos" is clarified in the book "Future Navigators on the Edge of Forever", ISBN; 978-1-36-662145-0.

"Other thinkers have entered the notion with some obvious contradictions. The following is from Frank J. Tipler a mathematical physicist. The work 'Omega Point Cosmology' in title."

"Frank Tipler generalizes Teilhard's term Omega Point to describe what he maintains is the ultimate fate of the universe required by the laws of physics: Roughly, Tipler argues that quantum mechanics is inconsistent unless the future of every point in space-time contains an intelligent observer to collapse the wave-function, and that the only way for this to happen is if the Universe is closed (that is, it will collapse to a single point) and yet contains observers with a 'God-like' ability to perform an unbounded series of observations in finite time."

"However, scientists such as Lawrence Krauss have stated that Tipler's reasoning is erroneous on multiple levels, possibly to the point of being nonsensical pseudoscience."

"By 1962, The Society of Jesus had strayed from Spanish Jesuit Priest Francisco Suarez's philosophies on Man in favor of Teilhardian 'evolutionary cosmogenesis.

"Teilhard's Christ is the 'Cosmic Christ' or the 'Omega' of revelation. He is an emanation of God which is made of matter and experienced the nature of evolution by being born into this world and dying. His resurrection from the dead was not to heaven, but to the noosphere, the area of convergence of all spirituality and spiritual beings, where Christ will be waiting at the end of time."

"When the earth reaches its Omega Point, everything that exists will become one with divinity."

"As said, Teilhard's theory was a personal attempt in creating a new Christianity in which science and theology coexist. The outcome was that his theory of the Omega Point was not perfectly scientific as examined by physicists, and not perfectly Christian either."

"There are, of course, more modern hypothesis, such as that of the 'Accelerating Expansion of the Universe'. In 1998, a value measured from observations of Type IA supernovae seemed to indicate that what was once assumed to be temporary cosmological expansion was actually accelerating! The apparent acceleration has caused many to dismiss Omega Point out of hand, since the necessity of a final big crunch singularity is key to the Omega Point's workability (although a big crunch-final singularity is still required under many current space- time theoretical models)."

"In addition to such models, there is the idea of technological singularity. The technological singularity is the hypothetical advent of artificial general intelligence theoretically capable of recursive self-improvement, resulting in a runaway effect to an intelligence explosion."

"Eric Steinhart, a proponent of 'Christian trans-humanism', argues there is significant overlap of ideas between the secular singularity and Teilhard's religious Omega Point."

"Steinhart quotes Ray Kurzweil, who stated that 'evolution moves inexorably toward our conception of God, albeit never reaching this ideal.' Like Kurzweil, Teilhard predicts a period of rapid technological change that results in a merger of humanity and technology. He believes that this marks the birth of the noosphere and the emergence of the spirit of the Earth. Teilhard's singularity is marked by the evolution of human intelligence reaching a critical point in which humans ascend from 'transhuman' to 'post-human'."

In its time, the above theories were of much interest and helped us to focus on the matter of the ending for human existence. Of course, in this time, we know that Space-Time has different dictates. It is the "Forever", the ultimate chemical-physical reality that holds all time past and present and offers a future of ever evolving universes. So, the Cosmos in one form or another is filled with lasting opportunity. Further, as we deepen our understanding of the chemical-physical vastness surrounding us, we have the opportunity to join that Cosmos in its everlasting context. That premise just the same means we must face certain realities. We have evolutionary and practical boundaries to cross!

The cold reality of existence in the surrounding cosmos and the aging of our earth (accelerated in our hands) creates a point, a final edge. This final edge is a TERMINUS, the possible end to humanity, a total death of the species. Or if it is approached in wisdom, it could lead to a wondrous, eternal existence!

Clearly, with the changes in our earth and the continuing evolution of the human form we must recognize that there will be that final boundary over which we must find a way to cross, or cease to exist.

How wonderful it would be that the best within us, the remarkable human, could advance into the far future realm of the stars!

CHAPTER 2: JUST INSIDE

How Did We Get to Here?

OK, that points out the possibilities of the far future, that is, closed in one case as an evolving total no longer human entity and open in others as singular mentalities capable of crossing beyond into the forever cosmos. But is it even worth troubling about, that is, our "Lasting Ability"?

 Well, let's first back up…. in fact, we are, indeed, rather "very special"! We come out of dust with an awesome and unique capability that we have not yet discovered elsewhere in space-time!

Rising from the Dust
Curious, isn't it? When you really look at life, for example, the absolutely beautiful and miraculous corals and the huge islands they formed from their metabolism …And look at us! My goodness creatures with just enough structure to support an incredible super-creative billion cell central processing unit!

So, located here on this earth we are wont to ask, how did we get here and what makes us different from the other creatures that inhabit our incredible plant. Does cosmic dust contain the building blocks for making DNA? And how different is our DNA from other living things?

Again, you ask, why bother with this? Well, unless we understand how delicately precious, we are, we may not worry about where it is all going in the future for those that we create ourselves. Yes, that is our children and theirs!

It turns out that the subject is properly entitled: "The Building Blocks of Life May Have Come from Outer Space". It is and has been worthy of the inquiry of many prominent scientists. S, we must go deeper into matter, which is first addressed by Ker Than in the following.

3.___ "Ever since the discovery of organic molecules in a meteorite that landed in Australia about half a century ago, scientists have been tantalized by the possibility that the building blocks of life originated in space. New research is shedding light on how such compounds might have formed and found their way to Earth."

"Fred Ciesla, who is a planetary scientist at the University of Chicago, and Scott Sanford, a NASA astrophysicist, say that our solar system was on the fast track to create life before Earth existed. These scientists made a computer model of the solar nebula—the disk of gas and dust from which the Sun and planets formed 4.6 billion years ago. The primordial debris included icy grains containing frozen water, ammonia, and carbon dioxide, among other molecules."

"Ciesla and Sanford simulated the movements of 5,000 (nitrogen containing carbonized) ice grains over a million years in the turbulence of the solar nebula. 'Which tossed them about like laundry in a dryer, lofting some high enough so that they were being irradiated directly by the young Sun', says Ciesla. High-energy ultraviolet radiation broke molecular bonds, creating highly reactive atoms that were prone to recombine and form more stable— and sometimes, more complex—compounds."

"Ciesla and Sanford say that this process could have generated organic molecules such as amino acids, amphiphiles and nucleobases—the building blocks of proteins, cell membranes and RNA and DNA, respectively. Some of these organic molecules found their way to small rocky bodies— planetesimals—that littered the early solar system. Those, in turn, combined to form comets, asteroids and planets, including ours. Thus, young Earth Ciesla theorizes was infused with organic molecules fabricated in space. Additional organic compounds, he suggests, could have formed later in Earth's primordial soup, or were delivered to our planet by comets and meteorites."

"Rebecca Martin, who is a NASA Sagan Fellow from the University of Colorado, says that the odds of meteorites reaching Earth got a boost from

Jupiter. And astronomer Mario Livio of the Space Telescope Science Institute in Baltimore says that when the solar system was forming, Jupiter's gravity prevented nearby planetesimals from coalescing. The bodies smashed into one another, breaking into fragments that settled into an asteroid belt 158 million miles from Earth. If a young Jupiter had passed through the belt while settling into its orbit around the Sun, it would have scattered the asteroids; If its orbit had been too far from the belt, the asteroids would have accumulated and constantly bombarded the Earth, rendering it lifeless. Instead, the asteroid belt provided just the right number of asteroids to courier compounds to Earth without pounding it into oblivion."

"Both studies point to the possibility of life on other planets. Ciesla says that ii the process that we describe did play a role in the formation of the organics that we see in meteorites, then we expect basically every solar system to contain organics. However, only 4 percent of the known solar systems in our galaxy possess a Jupiter-type planet in the right place to create an asteroid belt like ours. There could be more asteroid belts out there Rebecca Martin indicates, but we just can't see them yet."

Nonetheless, here we are very probably seeded from the most elementary of cosmic material. Again, the reason for so tracing tells us that we-so much further developed from those building materials are incredibly precious, but as one must say fallible-subject to the powerful forces around us. These chemical-dynamic forces can allow us or simply detach us from ourselves molecule for molecule!

Even so, from dust to creature to animal to us, one must find the complete "WE". An article via John Noble Wilford takes up that subject.

4._ "He notes that they were flaking crude stone tools by 2.5 million years ago. Then some of them spread from Africa into Asia and Europe after two million years ago."

"With somewhat less certainty, most scientists think that people who look like us --- anatomically modern Homo sapiens --- evolved by at least 130,000 years ago, from ancestors who had remained in Africa. Their brain had reached today's size. They, too, moved out of Africa and eventually replaced nonmodern human species, notably the Neanderthals in Europe and parts of Asia, and Homo erectus, typified by Java Man and Peking Man fossils in the Far East."

"But agreement breaks down completely on the question of when, where and how these anatomically modern humans began to manifest creative and symbolic thinking. That is, *when did they become fully human in behavior as well as a body? When and where was human culture born?"*

Continuing….

"Dr. John E. Yellen an archaeologist with the National Science Foundation, observed that it is the hot issue, and we all have different positions. For much of the last century, archaeologists thought that modern behavior flowered relatively recently, 40,000 years ago, and only after Homo sapiens had pushed into Europe. They based their theory of a 'creative explosion' on evidence like the magnificent cave paintings in Lascaux and Chauvet."

"But some rebellious researchers suspected that this theory was a relic one in a time when their discipline was ruled by Eurocentrism. Archaeologists, the rebels contended, were simply not looking for earlier creativity in the right places."

"Several recent discoveries in Africa and the Middle East are providing the first physical evidence to support an older, more gradual evolution of modern behavior, one not centered in Europe. But other scientists, beyond acknowledging a few early sparks in Africa, remain unconvinced. One prominent researcher is putting forward a new hypothesis of genetic change to explain a more recent and abrupt appearance of creativity."

"The debate has never been so intense over what archaeologists see as the 'Dawn of Human Culture'."

"Dr. Clive Gamble, director of the Center for the Archaeology of Human Origins at the University of Southampton in England has said that Europe is a little peninsula that happens to have a large amount of spectacular archaeology, but the European grip of having all the evidence is beginning to slip. We're finding the wonderful new evidence in Africa and other places. And in the last two or three years, this has changed and widened the debate over modern human behavior."

"The uncertainty and confusion over the origin of modern cultural behavior stem from what appears to be a great time lag between the point when the species first looked modern and when it acted modern. Perhaps the first modern Homo sapiens emerged with a capacity for modern creativity, but it remained latent until needed for survival."

"Dr. Sally McBrearty, an anthropologist at the University of Connecticut believes the earliest Homo sapiens probably had the cognitive capability to invent Sputnik, but they didn't yet have the history of an invention or a need for those things. Perhaps the need arose gradually in response to the stresses of new social conditions, the environmental change or competition from nonmodern human species. Or perhaps the capacity for modern behavior came late, a result of some as yet undetected genetic transformation."

"Dr. Mary C. Stiner, an archaeologist at the University of Arizona, argues that those contrasting views, or variations of them, could be reduced to this single question: Was there some fundamental shift in brain wiring or some change in conditions of life?"

5._ That premise is examined in the "Dawn of Creativity".

The Sudden Genetic Advance

"The foremost proponent of the traditional theory that human creativity appeared suddenly and mainly in Europe is Dr. Richard G. Klein, a Stanford archaeologist. He describes his reasoning in a new book, 'The Dawn of Creativity', written with Blake Edgar and in a publication by John Wiley."

"Arguably, the 'dawn' was the most significant prehistoric event that archaeologists will ever detect the authors write including the following."

"Before it, human anatomical and behavioral change proceeded very slowly more or less hand in hand. Afterward, the human form remained remarkably stable, while behavioral change accelerated dramatically. In the space of less than about 40,000 years, ever more closely packed cultural 'revolutions' have taken humanity from the status of a relatively rare large mammal to something more like a geologic force."

"In that view, 40,000 years ago was the turning point in human creativity, when modern Homo sapiens arrived in Europe and left the first unambiguous artifacts of abstract and symbolic thought. They were making more advanced tools, burying their dead with ceremony, and expressing a new kind of self-awareness with beads and pendants for body ornamentation and in finely wrought figurines of the female form. As time passed, they projected on cave walls something of their lives and minds in splendid paintings of deer, horses, and wild bulls."

"As an explanation for this apparently abrupt flowering of creativity, Dr. Klein has proposed a neurological hypothesis. He notes that about 50,000 years ago a chance genetic mutation in effect rewired the brain in some critical way, possibly allowing for a significant advance in speech. The origin of human speech is another of evolution's mysteries. Improved communications at this time, in his view, could have enabled people to conceive and model complex natural and social circumstances and thus give them the fully modern ability to invent and manipulate culture."

"Although this transformation, with the genetic change leading to the behavioral change, occurred in Africa, Dr. Klein observed that it allowed human populations to colonize new and challenging environments."

"On reaching Europe, the rewired modern humans, called specifically 'Cro-Magnon', presumably outsmarted the resident Neanderthals, driving them to extinction by 30,000 years ago and leaving their indelible cultural mark on the land."

Dr. Klein concedes that the idea fails one important measure of a proper scientific hypothesis.

"It cannot be assessed or falsified by experiment or by examination of relevant human fossils. Skulls from that time show no change in brain size and are highly unlikely to show a genetic change in the brain's functioning. Although he considers the idea the most straightforward explanation, critics object that such a concept of an abrupt 'human revolution is too simplistic, as well as being unprovable."

"Besides, other archaeologists think it misguided to key interpretations so closely to the Cro-Magnon creative explosion, dazzling as it was. Such thinking might have been understandable, they say, when few archaeologists had investigated earlier sites elsewhere, and the little they found could not- and still cannot-match the artistic magnificence of Lascaux and Chauvet."

So, postulations continued as follows.

The Blombos Discoveries

"The Eurocentrism of old may have sown the seeds of its demise. Dr. Yellen wife of Dr. Brooks pointed out, the increasing research into the origins of modern behavior has been driven in part by a lively interest in explaining the source and nature of Cro-Magnon superiority in overwhelming the Neanderthals."

"In the last 30 years, scientists have learned that the Cro-Magnons originated in Africa and the Neanderthals seem to have evolved exclusively in Europe. So, archaeologists have begun searching more diligently in Africa for what they generally agree are attributes of early modern behavior like more complex stone technology, the introduction of tools made of bone, long-distance trade, a more varied diet, self-ornamentation, and abstract designs carved on tools and ocher."

"In a comprehensive study two years ago, Dr. McBrearty at the University of Connecticut and Dr. Alison S. Brooks of George Washington University said that the many artifacts indicative of modern behavior in Africa did not occur suddenly together, as predicted by the human revolution model, but at sites that are widely separated in space and time. This suggests, a gradual assembling of the package of modern human behaviors in Africa and its later export to other regions of the Old World."

"Exploring a cave at the southern tip of Africa, for example, Dr. Christopher Henshilwood of the South African Museum in Cape Town found evidence that the anatomically modern people there were turning animal bones into awls and finely polished weapon points more than 70,000 years ago."

"The skill for making such bone tools is considered more advanced in concept and application than that required in producing the usual stone tools.
Three weapon points, in particular, appear to have been shaped first with a stone blade and then polished, probably with a piece of leather and a mineral powder."

"From this Henshilwood noted why are they so finely polished?' It's actually unnecessary for projectile points to be so carefully made. It suggests to us that this is an expression of symbolic thinking. The people then said, 'Let's make a really beautiful object. "

Symbolic thinking

"Symbolic thinking, scientists explain, is a form of consciousness that extends beyond the here and now to a contemplation of the past and future and a perception of the world within and beyond one individual. Thinking and communicating through abstract symbols is the foundation of all creativity, art and music, language and, more recently, mathematics, science, and the written word."

"Henshilwood reported details of an even more striking 77,000-year-old find at the Blombos Cave site. Two small pieces of ocher, a soft red iron oxide looking stone, had been inscribed with crisscrossed triangles and horizontal lines. The decoration, made by the same cave dwellers, was more evidence, the archaeologist said, that 'we're pushing back the date of symbolic thinking in modern humans — far, far back."

"Previous excavations in the Katanda region of the Congo yielded barbed harpoon points carved out of bone 80,000 to 90,000 years ago. Dr. Brooks and Dr. Yelle, found that these ancient people not only possessed considerable technological capabilities at this time but also incorporated symbolic or stylistic content into their projectile forms."

As it turns out, the dating of the Blombos discoveries, once suspect, is now generally accepted by other archaeologists. But a few have challenged the interpretations. If the artifacts are really that old and represent a basic change in human culture, why are they not showing up all over?

"Noting that no similar artifacts had been found in at least 30 other sites in the region of Blombos, Dr. Klein said that the unique find did not justify a revision of ideas about when and where modern behavior began."

"Dr. Yellen disagrees agreed indicating that the population of modern Homo sapiens then was small and probably widely scattered and so ideas and cultural practices might have been slow to travel among different groups.

"Yellen observed that trying to start a fire with too little tinder you make sparks. But it takes a certain density of the stuff before the fire is going to catch and go somewhere. So, when you don't have other people in your face, you probably won't get or don't need the richness of behavior that came later."

The Social Factor

Even so, variations on this theme are offered in other attempts to explain scattered finds suggesting the presence of modern cultural behavior outside Europe before the Cro-Magnon efflorescence.

"Dr. Stiner and her husband, Dr. Steven L. Kuhn, both archaeologists at the University of Arizona, reported that their research in Turkey and Lebanon showed that people around 43,000 years ago were making and wearing strings of beads and shell ornaments of highly repetitive designs. Some shells were relatively rare marine varieties, luminous white or brightly colored. The bone of an eagle or vulture was incised for suspension as a pendant."

"These were presumably objects bearing some social communication, readily conveying information about kinship, status, and other aspects of identity to outsiders."

"Stiner said that ornamentation is universal among all modern human foragers, not to mention in complex societies that send social signals with wedding rings, designer clothes and hot-label sneakers."

"At the Mediterranean coastal dig sites of the Ucagizli Cave in Turkey and Knar Ail in Lebanon, in the corridor of migrations into Eurasia, the two archaeologists also found remains of animal bones, indicating a marked change in diet over time. The people there were eating fewer deer, wild cattle, and other large animals. They seemed to be hunting and gathering fewer of the slow-reproducing and easy-to-catch animals like shellfish and tortoises and more of the agile animals like birds and hares."

"Their living conditions had changed, Dr. Stiner and Dr. Kuhn surmised, and one cause could have been population increases that pressured their resources. Not that the region suddenly teemed with people, but where populations had been sparse, even modest increases could double or triple their numbers, forcing them to turn to lower-ranked food sources."

"Families and groups would be living in closer proximity, with more occasions to interact, which could account for the creation of so many body ornaments as part of a shared system of communication, signaling from afar to outsiders one's group identity and social status. Expressions of who you are had become much more important according to Stiner."

"In a report in June in The Proceedings of the National Academy of Sciences, the two archaeologists noted that this habitual production and use of standardized ornaments first appeared at about the same time at two other widely separated sites, in Kenya and Bulgaria. That implied the existence of certain cognitive capacities and that these evolved relatively late in prehistory, but they were probably not a consequence of a sudden genetic mutation."

"The fact that traditions of ornament making emerged almost simultaneously in the earliest Upper Paleolithic/Late Stone Age on three continents argues strongly against their corresponding to a specific event in the cognitive evolution of a single population", said Dr. Stiner.

In the book "The Future Navigator", by D.M. Yourtee puts forward a simpler concept that ties all the various observations together. As all gradual mutations, DNA adjusts given the need for survival. The size of the brain is not so relevant as the amount and mutational character of DNA, contained. Thus, thoughtful based DNA will grow and could do so in various human forms and in various times and places.

Is DNA adjustment real. Of course, it is. For example, the numbers of liver enzymes for digestion, have extensively multiplied as human diets have increased in complication, and consider that Einstein's brain was normal size, but the DNA character contained in the available space was surely refined in a more inciteful way.

OK, so our dust got here, and we eventually were formed and developed highly analytical and very importantly social brains, but in a few individuals so what?

We had to produce more to make a voting majority. That does beg a basic question. What instinct caused early hominids to mate? When did humans recognize that coitus leads to new humans? There were certainly times when less population would have been more efficient for survival, but that did not happen. So, the billions formed and competed.

6._ This coitally based situation was addressed by J. Bryan Lowder as follows: "Two volunteers, an 18-year-old woman, and a 24-year-old man, dressed as cavemen are pictured in a cage of the Warsaw Zoo in 2009. (Warsaw's zoo has opened a new display where two volunteers dressed as cavemen will spend time in a former monkey-cage, to remind visitors that humans are animals too."

"When the 'Explainer' asked people to vote on a favorite unanswered question, the majority opted for a rather lascivious query regarding why rich ladies sunbathe topless, (and the Explainer has duly delivered your pound of flesh)."

"But in perusing the runners-up, another question so intrigued the Explainer that he could not resist answering it as well."

"When and how did humankind figure out that sex is what causes babies? It's not exactly the most obvious correlation: Sex doesn't always lead to babies, and there's a long lead time between the act and the consequences—weeks before there are even symptoms, usually. So roughly where do we think we were as a species when it clicked?"

"Basically, since the beginning! While anthropologists and evolutionary biologists can't be precise, all available evidence suggests that humans have understood that there is some relationship between copulation and childbirth since Homo sapiens first exhibited greater cognitive development, sometime between the emergence of our species 200,000 years ago and the elaboration of human culture probably about 50,000 years ago."

"Material evidence for this knowledge is thin, but one plaque from the Çatalhöyük archaeological site seems to demonstrate that a Neolithic understanding, with two figures embracing on one side and a mother and child depicted on the other. A firmer conclusion can be drawn from the fact that, though explanations for conception vary wildly across contemporary cultural groups, everyone acknowledges at least a partial link between sex and babies."

7._ As for how humans attained what biological anthropologist Holly Dunsworth calls "reproductive consciousness," that part is murkier.

"Most likely, we got the gist from observing animal reproduction cycles and generally noting that women who do not sleep with men do not get pregnant. But that doesn't mean that early peoples—or for that matter, modern people—thought or think of the process in the utilitarian, sperm-meets-egg way that the scientifically literate do now."

"Around the turn of the 20th century, anthropologists working in places such as Australia and New Guinea reported that their subjects did not recognize a connection between sex and children. However, subsequent research has shown these biased reports to be only half-true at best. For example, Bronislaw Malinowski claimed in 1927 that, for Trobriand Islanders, the father played no role in producing a child. But later anthropologists studying the same group learned that semen was believed to be necessary for the "coagulation" of menstrual blood, the stoppage of which was thought to eventually form the fetus."

"Even though the Trobriand Islanders' traditional explanations of conception seem quaint or strange, they do on some level recognize the tie between sex and childbirth."

"And of course, before we westerners get to feeling all superior, it must be said that our notions of conception are not wholly consistent or rational either. (The number of unplanned pregnancies in the United States reveals as much.)"

"As women's studies scholar Cynthia Eller points out, while other events may also be necessary—such as the entrance of a spirit child through the top of the head (in the case of the Triobriand Islanders), or the entrance of a soul into a fertilized egg (in the case of Roman Catholics) it is simply not believed that women bear children without any male participation whatsoever."

"If we humans have essentially always kind of understood that the deed usually leads to the delivery room, did that knowledge have any consequences on our evolution as a society? "

"Dunsworth argues that of the vast entire animal world, reproductive consciousness is unique to humans. That special knowledge may help explain both the evolution of our taboos around sex and our efforts to bend nature's procreative capacities to our favor in everything from dog-breeding to family planning."

Yet, this is a most worthy point, with the still remaining reproductive growing totality of humanity the WE, must strain the inner feelings of sympathy for each other!

Number of People Who Have Ever Lived

Clearly, from star dust there has resulted the basic "WE" on the way to the future. This begs the question, what is the number of people who have ever lived, that is. what have we been forced to push against?

8.___The answer is in an updated version of one of the most popular features on PRB's website, estimating the number of people who have ever been born. Estimates were first made in 1995, with updates in 2002 and 2011, and 2017.

"Modern Homo sapiens (that is, people who were roughly like we are now) first walked the Earth about 50,000 years ago. Since then, more than 108 billion members of our species have ever been born, according to estimates by Population Reference Bureau (PRB). Given the current global population of about 7.5 billion (based on our most recent estimate as of mid-2017), that means those of us currently alive represent about 7 percent of the total number of humans who have *ever lived.*"

In net, we got here –as gathered space dust- grew into a socially connected animal DNA adjusting to those demands and figured out how to increase our population. And, with but a thumb and upright posture figured out how to survive on this complicated planet with hurricanes, tornados, blizzards, volcanos, and vast oceans between destinations, etc.

In a nutshell there is an absolute incredible nature to our present existence. With humble body and the power of our brains, we have shown we can survive, at least within the past and slowly changing...current world.

As said at the beginning of this chapter--- in point of fact we are rather "Very Special"!

Worth continuing?

CHAPTER 3: FORTUNE WITHIN

Are We Truly Sufficiently Gifted?

Well, so here now is the "WE", surviving over time in the billions, with about seven plus billion here today.

WE came from the dust of space and evolved- surviving in such remarkable numbers. Why? Our bodies are full of foibles and under duress have very true earthly limits---we are if you will fundamentally weak for a place that can sweep you away with the wind or freeze you to death in the snow!

Well, all life structures here are built on DNA. For that matter, and to choose comparison, how different are we from all the other creatures on planet earth in that critical nucleic acid regard.

Let's begin at a "Basic" level. How different is the DNA from Human and other simple living things? This introduction is aided by John Noble Wilford.

9._ "The difference between Animal DNA and Plant DNA is how the four nucleotides in DNA are arranged. It's their sequence that determines which proteins will be made. The way the nucleotides are arranged, and the information they encode, decides whether the organism will produce scales or leaves – legs or a stalk."

"Research shows that plants and animals may produce some proteins in common. For example, a protein called Cytochrome C. As the DNA copying process is imperfect and because of mistakes accumulated over time, Cytochrome C is slightly different in various creatures. The gene regions that specify the amino acid sequence in human Cytochrome C are more similar to those in another mammal like a rabbit, and less similar to a more distant creature, like a sunflower."

"In addition, there are differences in the size of the genomes as plants tend to have larger genomes and are often polyploid. Ploidy refers to the basic number of unique chromosomes in the genome. Every species has a characteristic number of chromosomes, called the chromosome number. Animals tend to have more chromosomes while plants have fewer."

"Lastly, at a more detailed level, there can be certain subtle differences. The genes encoded by DNA can be regulated by chemical modifications such as methylation. The specific modifications can vary from tissue to tissue within the same animal or from organism to organism. Some animals, such as a nematode worm known as Caenorhabditis elegans, do not seem to have DNA methylation. Differences in DNA methylation patterns are not specifically attributable to differences between animals and plants: variations also occur in different types of animals or even in different tissues within the same animal."

So, all in all among life forms on earth we are both different and a bit the same. Even so, how much different, and so what if there is a difference?

Clearly that begs the next question. What ape is closest to humans, what is the difference, and what is their relative capability? Let's consider the Bonobos Chimps. We peek in through an article by Ann Gibbons.

10._ "Chimpanzees now have to share the distinction of being our closest living relative in the animal kingdom. An international team of researchers has sequenced the genome of the bonobo for the first time, confirming that it shares the same percentage of its DNA with us as chimps do. The team also found some small but tantalizing differences in the genomes of the three species—differences that may explain how bonobos and chimpanzees don't look or act like us even though we share about 99% of our DNA."

"Janet Kelso of the Max Planck Institute for Evolutionary Anthropology in Leipzig, Germany a computational biologist puts it this way. We're so closely related genetically, yet our behavior is so different."

"This will allow us to look for the genetic basis of what makes our modern humans different from both bonobos and chimpanzees."

"Ever since researchers sequenced the chimp genome in 2005, they have known that humans share about 99% of our DNA with chimpanzees, making them our closest living relatives. But there are actually two species of apes that are this closely related to humans: bonobos (Pan paniscus) and, yes, the common chimpanzee (Pan troglodytes). This has prompted researchers to speculate whether the ancestor of humans, chimpanzees, and bonobos looked and acted more like a bonobo, a chimpanzee, or something else—and how all three species have evolved differently since the ancestor of humans split with the common ancestor of bonobos and chimps between 4 million and 7 million years ago in Africa."

"The international sequencing effort led from Max Planck chose a bonobo named Ulindi from the Leipzig Zoo as its subject, partly because she was a female (the chimp genome was of a male). The analysis of Ulindi's complete genome, reported online today in Nature, reveals that bonobos and chimpanzees share 99.6% of their DNA. This confirms that these two species of African apes are still highly similar to each other genetically, even though their populations split apart in Africa about 1 million years ago, perhaps after the Congo River formed and divided an ancestral population into two groups. Today, bonobos are found in only the Democratic Republic of Congo and there is no evidence that they have interbred with chimpanzees in equatorial Africa since they diverged, perhaps because the Congo River acted as a barrier to prevent the groups from mixing. The researchers also found that bonobos share about 98.7% of their DNA with humans—about the same amount that chimps share with us."

"When the Max Planck scientists compared the bonobo genome directly with that of chimps and humans, however, they found that a small bit of our DNA, about 1.6%, is shared with only the bonobo, but not chimpanzees. And we share about the same amount of our DNA with only chimps, but not bonobos."

"These differences suggest that the ancestral population of apes that gave rise to humans, chimps, and bonobos was quite large and diverse genetically—numbering about 27,000 breeding individuals. Once the ancestors of humans split from the ancestor of bonobos and chimps more than 4 million years ago, the common ancestor of bonobos and chimps retained this diversity until their population completely split into two groups 1 million years ago. The groups that evolved into bonobos, chimps, and humans all retained slightly different subsets of this ancestral population's diverse gene pool—and those differences now offer clues today to the size and range of diversity in that ancestral group."

"While the function of the small differences in DNA in the three lineages today is not yet known, the Max Planck team sees clues that some may be involved in parts of the genome that regulate immune responses, tumor suppression genes, and perception of social cues. "

"The common chimpanzee, for example, shows selection for a version of a gene that may be involved in fighting retroviruses, such as HIV—a genetic variant not found in humans or bonobos, which may explain why chimps get a milder strain of HIV (called simian immunodeficiency virus) than humans do."

"Another difference is that bonobos and humans, but not chimps, have a version of a protein found in urine that may have similar function in apes as it does in mice, which detect differences in scent to pick up social cues."

"Molecular anthropologist Maryellen Ruvolo of Harvard University, who was not involved in the work points out that this paper is a significant benchmark achievement that lays the groundwork for other types of investigations into Homo-Pan differences. As researchers study the genome in more depth, they hope to find the genetic differences that make bonobos more playful than chimps, for example, or humans more cerebral. The bonobo genome also should put to rest arguments that humans are more closely related to chimps, says primatologist Frans de Waal of Emory University in Atlanta. An

De Waal commented that the story that the bonobo can be safely ignored or marginalized from debates about human origins is now off the

It is noted the updated article shows that chimps and bonobos are two species of chimpanzees that are close enough to humans to share 99.6% of their DNA. The researchers also found that the ancestors of humans split from the ancestor of bonobos and chimps more than 4 million years ago.

So here it is in terms of DNA that 0.4% DNA difference may have led to a species (us) that is in its instructions more in social analytical sensitivity (and some better handing and running ability.) Hence when that special gift, social work--- works--- we work to survive in spite of more than just a few challenges.

Viva la difference! That may be (in a chemical sense) what caused humans to be smarter than animals as example the Chimp? Even so, a bit more digging is needed to clarify. Why, indeed. At the practice level, are humans so much "smarter" than animals?

Continuing the forgoing article … "Such a simple question. Many of you might think. Has that question really disappeared?" Some questions disappear forever because they have been answered. Some questions go extinct because they were bad questions to begin with. But there are others that appear to vanish but then we find that they are back with us again in a slightly different guise. They are questions that are just too close to our hearts for us to let them die completely."

"For millennia, human superiority was taken for granted. From the lowest forms of life up to humans and then on to the angels and God, all living thing were seen as arranged in the Great Chain of Being. Ascend the chain and perfection grows. It is a hierarchical philosophy that conveniently allows for the exploitation of dumber beasts — of other species or races — as a right by their superiors. We dispose of them as God disposes of us."

"The idea of human superiority should have died when Darwin came on the scene. Unfortunately, the full implications of what he said have been difficult to take in: there is no Great Chain of Being, no higher and no lower. All creatures have adapted effectively to their own environments in their own way. Human "smartness" is just a particular survival strategy among many others, not the top of a long ladder."

"It took a surprisingly long time for scientists to grasp this. For decades, comparative psychologists tried to work out the learning abilities of different species so that they could be arranged on a single scale. Animal equivalents of intelligence tests were used, and people seriously asked whether fish were smarter than birds."

"It took the new science of ethology, created by Nobel-prize winners Konrad Lorenz, Niko Tinbergen and Karl von Frisch, to show that each species had the abilities it needed for its own lifestyle, and they could not, be not arranged on a universal scale. "

So, using just a broad term of comparison Human smartness is no smarter than anyone else's smartness.

The problem here is what is "smartness". Obviously, some animals are able to survive in conditions we can't. Thus, the topic needs a bigger dig in. To continue with the commentary by these scientists...

"Artificial intelligence researchers came along later but they too could not easily part from medieval thinking. The most important problems to tackle were agreed to be those that represented our 'highest' abilities. Solve them and everything else would be easy. As a result, we have ended up with computer programs that can play chess as well as a grandmaster. But, unfortunately. we have none that can make a robot walk *(just)* as well as a 2-year old, yet alone run like a cat."

"Strangely enough, even evolutionary biologists still get caught up with the notion that humans stand at the apex of existence. There are endless books from evolutionary biologists speculating on the reasons why humans evolved such wonderful big brains, but a complete absence of those which ask if a big brain is a really useful organ to have. The evidence is far from persuasive. If you look at a wide range of organisms, those with bigger brains are generally no more successful than those with smaller brains—they go extinct just as fast."

"Of course, it would be really nice to sample a large range of different planets where life is to be found and see if big-brained creatures do better over really long-time scales (the Earth is quite a young place). Unfortunately, we cannot yet do that, although the fact that we have never been contacted by any intelligent life from older parts of the Universe suggests that it usually comes to a bad end."

OK, Still, as we are humans it's just so hard not to be seduced by the question 'What makes us so special' which is just the same as the question above but in a different form.

"When you switch on a kitchen light and see a cockroach scuttle for safety, you can't help seeing it as a lower form of life. Unfortunately, there are a lot more of them than there are of us, and they have been around far, far longer. Cockroach philosophers doubtless entertain their six-legged friends by asking 'What makes us so special'."

"Like many a scholar before and since, Bertrand Russell confidently asserts that certain traits as 'speech, fire, agriculture, writing, tools, and large-scale cooperation'—set humans apart from animals. Although we appear to excel in many domains, such claims are not typically founded in any thorough comparison. In fact, if you set the bar low, you can conclude that parrots can speak, ants have agriculture, crows make tools, and bees cooperate on a large scale."

"We need to dig deeper to understand to what we owe our unique success—what separates us from other animals in the domains of language, mental time travel, theory of mind, intelligence, culture, and morality. In each domain, various nonhuman species have competences, but human ability is special in some respects—and they have much in common."

"In all six domains there are found repeatedly <u>two major features that set us apart: our open-ended ability to imagine and reflect on different situations, and our deep-seated drive to link our scenario-building minds together</u>."

"It seems to be primarily these two attributes that carried our ancestors across the gap, turning animal communication into open-ended human language, memory into mental time travel, social cognition into theory of mind, problem solving into abstract reasoning, social traditions into cumulative culture, and empathy into morality."

Michael Tomasello and colleagues belong in this discourse. Here are some unified thoughts. "Humans are avid scenario builders. We can tell stories, picture future situations, imagine others' experiences, contemplate potential explanations, plan how to teach, and reflect on moral dilemmas. Nested scenario building refers not to a single ability but to a complex faculty, itself built on a variety of sophisticated components that allow us to simulate and to reflect."

"A basic capacity to simulate seems to exist in other animals. When rats are in a well-known maze, the sequential firing of so-called place cells in the hippocampus suggests that the rats can cognitively sweep ahead, considering one path and then the other, before deciding about where to go. Appropriate place-cell sequences have also been recorded during sleep and rest, suggesting a neural basis for the learning of the maze layout and its options. The challenges of navigation may well have been selected for the fundamentals of mental scene construction. Moreover, great apes have demonstrated several other relevant capacities. They can think about hidden movements, learn, and interpret human symbols, solve some problems through mental rather than physical computation, have complex sociality and some traditions, console each other, recognize themselves in mirrors, and show signs of pretense in play and deception. Great apes have a basic capacity to imagine alternative mental scenarios of the world. In certain situations, their abilities are comparable to those of 18- to 24-month-old human children.

Even so, our ancestors discovered that they could dramatically improve the accuracy of their mental scenarios by increasingly connecting their minds to others."

"We give each other advice—for instance, by posting signs about the possible presence of crocodiles. We can broadcast our imaginary play not only throughout our own system but to others around us. We exchange our ideas and give feedback. We ask others, and we inform them—for instance, by recounting what it was like when we were in a similar situation. We take an interest even without knowing whether anything important or useful comes of it. There are individual differences in how much an interest people display in what certain others have to say, but we are generally driven to wire our minds to those around us. Our expectations and plans are subsequently a lot better than they could have been if we didn't listen. It is generally good advice to consider advice—preferably from a variety of sources before making up your own mind."

"Nested scenario builders can benefit from cooperating with other scenario builders in many other ways. For instance, our audience can be recruited for common goals. We can hatch complex plans, divide labor, and pledge cooperation. We can accumulate our achievements and pass them on to the next generation. To ensure all this happens, we appear to be hard-wired with an insatiable urge to connect our minds."

"Primates are social creatures, and evidence that social pressures have driven the evolution of primate intelligence is mounting. Humans have taken this sociality to another level. Unlike other primates, children sob to attract attention and sympathy. We ask what's wrong and try to make things better. We look each other in the eye, share what's on our minds, and absorb what is on the other's. This urge to connect must have been crucial to the establishment of signs and words that allow us to read others' minds and express our own."

As Michael Tomasello and colleagues have demonstrated, we make and pursue shared goals where our closest animal relatives do not! Therein lies the reason that those billions came along! Continuing with reinforcement...

"Even 2-year-old children outperform great apes on tasks of social learning, communication, and intention reading. Other animals may give alarm calls and food calls but otherwise do not show many signs of a drive to share their experience and knowledge with others. Again, in all six domains this cooperative drive is evident and plays a significant role. Language is the primary means by which we exchange our minds. We talk to each other about the past and make plans about the future. We read and tell each other what is on our minds. We reason and solve problems collectively. We build social narratives that explain the world around us. We teach, and we learn from each other. And we argue about what is right and what is wrong. These examples serve to remind us how pervasive the urge to connect is. Those who lack this drive have severe social difficulties (and may be diagnosed as autistic). Our urge to connect was essential for the creation of cumulative cultures that shape our minds and endow us with our impressive powers."

"Our capacity for nested scenario building even allows us, drawing on past experiences, to imagine others' advice internally. (Hearing voices is quite normal. Relax. The trouble starts when you attribute these internal voices to external sources.) So, you might ask yourself what your mother would have said about the situation you find yourself in. We care about whether our parents, friends, heroes, or gods would be proud of what we do, even if they no longer exist (or never did). We can consider what others might remember us for. These thoughts can be important drivers motivating us to go beyond satisfying immediate personal self-interests in pursuit of "higher" notions of honor, valor, and glory."

"We might aspire to nobility in character and virtue in action. We can invest heavily in unselfish actions, such as fighting oppression or pollution or helping a club, a person, or an animal. When we take on a cause, we seem to become part of something bigger and from such endeavors may derive some of the deepest feeling of meaning. One of the most remarkable things about humans is that we can strive to make some kind of difference. We may deliberately practice random acts of kindness, spread the word, fight injustice, teach the next generation, or start a revolution. Without the urge to connect our minds, such traits could not exist."

So that clears up a lot of confusion that has led to "rational uncertainty"

Yes, we are indeed quite a remarkable species, in that our brains function in a very connecting way as scenario builders-who react with special inquiry and survival creations.

This is not to forget that those brains are packed with a genetically transferable DNA that must have adapted to that scenario in order to accomplish the remarkable that we can and often do.

In sum, nested scenario building and the drive to link our scenario-building minds together turned ape qualities into human qualities. They created powerful feedback loops that dynamically changed much of the human condition. They carried us where other animals could not go!

Again, there is no other way to say it, we are beyond whatever should be, constructed with doing brains and exactly the right physiology and attitude to create survival places and prosper on the evolved. Earth.

But are we really superior, sufficiently gifted in the sense of lasting ability, in total predictive intelligence? **Well, we are right now in process of testing that!**

That is, there develops a totally nagging question. With so much gained, with so many favors from the stardust and our earth, why are we destined to suicide?

There is in front of us a boundary…that absolutely must be considered!

It is- we shall call it---the "Edge"--- that line which crossed over puts those crossing in a region directly before the "Final Boundary" the potential "Terminus" of humanity.

43

CHAPTER 4: TROUBLES WITHIN

Our Edge Behavior

So far "WE" are survivors for reasons of a brain-DNA serendipitous mutation yielding a special ability to think in an organized -community oriented way as detailed above. Viva la (that) difference!

Even so, our Central Control machinery seems to have some of us acting in low uncivilized, cruel animal like, uncommunicative and terminal behavior ways. Why? Is it something simple we have overlooked? Are some humans born with a lingering beast like psyche? The record on this is massively recorded, from brutal murders, to wars and torture, the literature, and daily reports on this is so huge that there is no need to provide extensive citation.

And, one can reach herein way out to get to the bottom of this. Following, is one recently digested example: We were raised as meat eaters. How does eating just killed animal flesh (from sushi to hamburger) affect a person's psyche?

Actually, the risks of eating meat are also recorded. Here is a personal account by a contributor and then scientific notations are presented from a widely distributed the World Health Organization (WHO) report.

"For as long as I can remember, I've been weirdly picky about meat — but I'm not really a vegetarian, either. My aversion to eating a lot of meat marked me as a giant weirdo back in the rural Midwest, but after researching what happens to your body when you eat meat - I'm more than a little pleased at my weird, semi-vegetarian status."

"If you're not big on meat either, you should know that's actually a good thing, because a new study from WHO claims that processed meat causes cancer and a myriad of health-related problems from an increased risk of colorectal cancer, hormone-sensitive breast cancer, diabetes, and Alzheimer's, to mental health issues such as depressive symptoms. Conversely, there's no denying that moderate consumption of meat (red or white) can provide your body with rich vitamins and nutrients such as B12 and protein."

"Apparently, even consuming 50 grams of processed meat daily (that's about the equivalent of two slices of lunch meat) can increase cancer risk in humans by 18 percent. Additionally, processed meat has officially been classified as carcinogenic to humans and unprocessed red meat may be as well. Evidently, while it is still said that red meat has some nutritional value, it appears that eating a lot of meat is not good for our health."

"To provide an overview of the knowledge on this matter---here is an enumeration of health effects - five things that happen to your body when you eat a lot of meat."

1. The Iron Levels in Your Brain Increase. 2. As said, you Raise Your Risk of Cancer. 3. Your Immune System Gets a Boost. 4. Your Blood Vessels & Arteries Harden. And in the context of this book's message, 5. Your Mood Suffers.

What was that last one? Yes, the mind and body are literally connected, and what we eat can seriously determine our mood, so it makes sense to talk about how eating meat can affect your mental state.

In a study published in The Nutrition Journal researchers found that restricting meat can improve the mood of modern omnivores in the short term. However, Of the three study groups, the one that avoided eating meat altogether showed the highest improvement in mood scores at the end of the study, whereas the omnivores who continued to eat meat throughout the study showed no significant changes in their mood scores.

That is, basically, if you are in a bad mood, it will continue if you keep at the meat. If you restrict it your mood improves. Well, a heck of a lot of detailed study would be needed to determine if this meat thing is relevant to un-mollified anger, but the point is once here we are susceptible to our way of acting through what we consume. The same applies to other-here in actual life- circumstances such as drug and alcohol abuse. There are certainly folks who have suffered panic attacks after ceasing to take a centrally acting mood control drug.

So, Humm… take away from these observations what you will (or need, the impact on the environment is extensively reported, and critically important) but after all of it, following is the real central salient observation.

In fact, the matter of basic interpersonal behavior has to reside in our brain DNA, and it is simply, and most likely that our brains are not implanted universally with empathy!

So, from that what is the result? Or to put it more directly where it counts, what is our record of support of each other through history*? Clearly, the depth of the way we care about each other is given in this question: How many humans have been killed in all the wars in human history?*

11. The data are easy to obtain from a wide variety of reliable sources on-line. Here is the gather data. In fact, of the past **3,400** years, humans have been entirely at peace for just 268 of them, or just 8 percent of recorded history! To this there are consequences…

"At least **108 million people** were killed in wars in the twentieth century. Estimates for the total number killed in wars throughout all of human history range from 150 million to 1 billion. In more detail…How many people have died from war? From Roberto Muehlenkam is this observation; "A total of about 1.64 billion people were killed by war (including deaths from famine and disease caused by war) throughout the history and prehistory of mankind."

"And to this, where benevolence should reside, Religious excuse has caused many notable killing wars to include The Crusades, The Inquisition, Northern Ireland (protestants versus catholic conflicts), the Middle East Muslin sect killings, 9/11 deaths in the US, Japan's Rising Sun in WW II, and need we name more?"

This is a matter of some consequence because faith should allow the empathy to arise, and there should never be a cause of killing. Clearly there are those who have committed horrendous acts based on religious zeal, and we while must be alert to these threats killing innocent people by other people enshrined in belief, is the fact. To this matter of "Troubles Within, Terminal-Edge Behavior" there is the question of support for the young, the new generations that face the Edge. There are many questions in this issue, but so important for the long term, is do the World's children have enough food and water? To help answer this question here is a list of useful facts and figures on world hunger (from WHO Reports).

- ✓ Some 795 million people in the world do not have enough food to lead a healthy active life. That's about one in nine people on earth.
- ✓ The vast majority of the world's hungry people live in developing countries, where 12.9 percent of the population is undernourished.
- ✓ Sub-Saharan Africa is the region with the highest prevalence (percentage of population) of hunger. One person in four there is undernourished. (Yes, that is one fourth of the population)
- ✓ Poor nutrition causes nearly half (45%) of deaths in children under five. *Yes, that is 3.1 million children each year!*
- ✓ One out of six children -- roughly 100 million -- in developing countries is underweight.
- ✓ One in four of the world's children are stunted. In developing countries, the proportion can rise to one in three.
- ✓ If women farmers had the same access to resources as men, the number of hungry in the world could be reduced by up to 150 million.
- ✓ 66 million primary school-age children attend classes hungry across the developing world, with 23 million in Africa alone.
- ✓ WFP calculates that US $3.2 billion is needed per year to reach all 66 million hungry school-age children.

These facts cause the lack of broad human empathy to glare at us, directly in the face! And, clearly the way we are sponsored to rise into adulthood is not working universally!

CHAPTER 5: WANTED WITHIN

Enrichment Potential

Even though some do not want others to live or at least are not concerned enough about them being killed-most of us do want to live! Clearly, there is something lacking in our birth-brains, and the way we reach adulthood.

So, what is the life (style) that most people want? Just how serious and difficult to achieve is that? Is it woven iron clad with lust, anger, and greed?

12._ Of all the things people indicated they want more of, the following were the 10 most frequently mentioned (via Dunsworth, et. al) by women. This is of course what men *should* help with.

The quotes below are from actual respondents, about what they perceive to be the biggest desires and challenges in the way of what they're longing for. Following each quote is the sociological-psychologists commentary.

#1: Happiness

Biggest challenge: "Not knowing what I want to do". This is the   #1 mentioned missing element-Happiness has become so hard to achieve, and even harder to maintain.

Comment; In my work with professional women, I've seen that happiness continually escapes them because, first, they don't really understand exactly what will make them happy. They just don't know themselves well at all.

Secondly, they search outside themselves for happiness - in a job, a husband, a family, a title, a paycheck, a fancy house. As a result, Happiness is constantly out of their control and a perpetual moving target that never stands still long enough for them to grasp. I'm not saying that these things don't bring happiness - of course, they can.

The key point is that if everything you're searching for remains outside of you, you'll always be scrambling and chasing.

#2: Money

Biggest challenge: "Not having enough money or time to accomplish the things I want to do."

Comment: I've collaborated with millionaires, as well as people who earn mid-six figures and far, far less. Isn't it fascinating that no matter what we earn, we somehow feel we never have enough? I know people with literally over a million dollars in their retirement accounts, yet they live in such a constant fear state around money that they never have a moment's peace. The question is: how much money do you really need to bring about the life experiences that will truly fulfill you? And if you want more money, do you understand the key principles and behaviors required to generate it?

#3: Freedom

Biggest challenge: "Having the freedom to find my 'true purpose' or being lit up by the day-to-day at work."

Comment: Ah, freedom. We all want it, yet so many people I meet are resistant to doing what's required to get it. They want to "feel" free, yet are scared to muster the courage to do what's necessary to "become" free.

What is necessary to experience freedom? I've seen that it requires making yourself right (not wrong), following your own authentic values and beliefs, and building strong boundaries to protect yourself from what others will tell you is right for you or try to force on you. And it takes forging your own path in life and work, despite the challenges and the nay-sayers.

It requires BOLDNESS and courage to make yourself your own highest authority on life and work, and that's no easy thing today. Sadly, most of us aren't taught or trained (particularly women) how to stand up powerfully for what we want and believe in, and to go after it with undying passion and commitment.

#4: Peace

Biggest challenge: "Lack of clarity about who I am and my purpose."

We long for peace, desperately. Peace from noise, chatter, pressure, responsibilities. We also want peace from the pain and thumping inside our own heads - the conflicts and strain we inflict on ourselves every minute to be better, stronger, smarter (prettier, thinner, better parents, _____[you fill in the blank]).

Peace, I've found, doesn't come from being better at anything, or even figuring anything out. Attaining peace is a practice that we need to cultivate and commit to. Peace today will never just fall in our laps - it's too chaotic a world. We have to carve out space within ourselves and in our lives to bring forward the experience of peace, then do the work to expand peace as a feeling and experience that we'll commit to daily, regardless of what's around us. You don't have to know your purpose to be at peace - you just have to commit to being at peace, and building daily practices that will support you in that commitment.

#5: Joy

Biggest challenge: "How to find the right role or position for me now that will bring joy in my work."

Comment; In working with thousands of women to build successful, rewarding careers they love, I've witnessed how the process of stepping up to our highest potential and honoring our best visions for contributing to the world in a meaningful way does indeed pave the way for more joy. I believe (and have lived) that we simply can't feel joy in our lives if the work we do pains us. We're not able to effectively separate who we are from what we do (and why would we want to?).

So, when you're stuck in work you hate, with people you don't respect, supporting outcomes that feel wrong to you, then your life as a whole can't help but be joyless, even if your personal or family life brings you happiness.

#6: Balance

Biggest challenge: "Balancing my need/desire for flexibility while making enough money and having the benefits I want."

Comment: I've researched work-life balance extensively, and believe that it's doable only under one condition: that you understand clearly what your top life priorities are, and you defend and honor those priorities fiercely, every minute of the day. It takes understanding your non-negotiables (what you won't compromise on, what you won't say "yes" to), and then living from that knowledge, and making the right decisions that align with your top life priorities. If you can't do that, you can't create or sustain balance.

#7: Fulfillment

Biggest challenge: "Utilizing my potential in the best possible way, for myself and for others."

Comment: Fulfillment can be defined as this: "Satisfaction or happiness as a result of fully developing one's abilities or character." We simply can't experience fulfillment if we're not living up to what we know is our highest and best potential. Have you ever settled for something much less than you know you want or deserve? It hurts - a lot.

But to live up to our highest potential, we have to leave our comfort zones behind, and perhaps even leave behind the definition we've crafted of who we think we are, and the stories we tell ourselves about what we're capable of, so that we can become the person we dream to be. We may also have to leave some people and relationships behind (the ones that don't support you to soar higher and grow because it threatens them).

Fulfillment is possible when you are filling up your cup, honoring your own potential, not forsaking yourself by putting everyone else in front of you. Fulfillment comes when you take bold actions that say "yes" to the future vision of you, even well before it's "hatched."

#8: Confidence

Biggest challenge: "Feeling like I have something to offer now, rather than feeling constantly as if I'm not ready and need more training."

Comment: I've seen in working with thousands of women over 10 years that we humans only see what's at the tip of our noses. And when we're in situations that are hurtful, demeaning, challenging and worse, we lose confidence. We get rocked. We forget who we are, and what we are capable of, and see only the boss in front of us who's yelling or the colleague who's tearing us down.

It's a tough world out there, but there are many ways we can stay true to our gifts and capabilities, and build our confidence. For that, we need support from others who believe in us without fail. We need to build our "tribe" of people who will do anything for us. And we need to believe in ourselves without fail, despite the evidence around us that says we're not "ready" to soar.

#9: Stability

Biggest challenge: "Figuring out what to do next, to keep me afloat and be a bridge to my later years and retirement."

Comment: I think that some of the worst advice many of us have ever received in life falls under the category of "Do the stable, secure thing!" As one who followed the "stable" path for 18 years, and pursued a corporate life that was, in the end, very wrong for me, I know that "stable" can be the kiss of death. After experiencing a brutal layoff in the days following 9/11, and feeling as if my whole life and career came crashing down around me, I now know this - NOTHING outside of us is "secure or stable."

Only YOU are stable - your spirit, your intelligence, your capabilities, your gifts and what you have to offer others and the world. And how you choose to react to what comes your way - that's what brings stability. These are the only aspects of life that are truly stable and secure in this world.

#10: Passion

Biggest challenge: "Overcoming feelings of ineptitude and negativity because of career setbacks."

Comment: Finally, passion - it seems that everyone talks about wanting to be passionate about their work. Yet passion is something that can demand a high price - the price of wrapping your entire entity around a certain direction (including risking your checkbook, your marriage and even your health) because you can't NOT pursue it.

What people often mean when they say "I want to feel passionate about my work" is this: They want to feel alive, not exhausted, beleaguered, and demoralized. They want to feel that there's a reason they're on this planet, a reason for the talents and abilities they were given at birth and have cultivated. They want to believe that they're here for a purpose and finding that purpose will give their lives the meaning and passion they're missing.

Passion can be tapped and uncorked, for sure, but only when you allow yourself to believe that your life and your work mean something more than merely existing for a paycheck, or doing the "secure" thing.

Well, all of that sets an important stage. Of course, it starts with healthy maturity.

Even so, What WE really want (aside from food and shelter) is frankly quite basic. And, as long as we recognize the security of balanced inner self, and the morality needed by self and others, it can be a good life. That, of course, is contingent upon the security of the world around us.

Ever so, much is occurring that will change human life over the next hundred years. Besieged by habitual killing and the ever-depreciating earth we must change morally for all in our global population.

We can with mutual will, capture the remaining time and change to something quite different. Then we may gain the universal strength to hold our earth and synchronize with the Cosmos' Forever.

An approach that will help ensure the happiness and success of people as the future unfolds, is given in Chapter 7. It involves the development from childhood to an adult of healthy unhindered- morally strengthened minds.

But, for now let's investigate what the future human could or is likely to be and even look like as we approach the "Edge", that margin leading to the Final Boundary. This is important because without enhancing the basic human our chances to challenge the Terminus- we will probably fall short.

Daniel Haug in "Getty Images" with other cited contributors helps us ponder the way we may look in forward time.

13._ "It's not really a biological question anymore, it's technological. Currently, people have implants to fix an element of the body that's broken, such as a pacemaker or a hip implant. Perhaps in the future, implants will be used simply to improve a person. As well as brain implants, we might have more visible parts of technology as an element of our appearance, such an artificial eye with a camera that can read different frequencies of color and visuals."

"We've all heard of designer babies. Scientists already have the technology to change the genes of an embryo though it's controversial and no one's sure what happens next. But in the future, Mailund suggests, 'it may be seen as unethical not to change certain genes.' With that may come choice about a baby's features, so perhaps humans will look like what their parents want them to look like."

This is all rather hypothetical and wades into some very argumentative territory, but can demographic trends give us any sense of what we may look like in the future?

Donald Lain Smith further in Getty asks will technology (indeed) affect our evolution or not?

"Predicting out a million years is pure speculation, but predicting into the more immediate future is certainly possible using bioinformatics by combining what is known about genetic variation now with models of demographic change going forward," says Dr. Jason A. Hodgson, Lecturer, Grand Challenges in Eco-systems, and the Environment.

"Now we have genetic samples of complete genomes from humans around the world, geneticists are getting a better understanding of genetic variation and how it's structured in a human population. We can't exactly predict how genetic variation will change, but scientists in the field of bioinformatics are looking to demographic trends to give us some idea."

Hodgson predicts that urban and rural areas will become increasingly differentiated within people. "All the migration comes from rural areas into cities so you get an increase in genetic diversity in cities and a decrease in rural areas," he said. "What you might see is differentiation along lines where people live."

14._ Ryan Deberardinis at EyeEm relays that "genetic diversity will increase in cities and decrease in rural areas. It will vary across the world but in the UK, for example, rural areas are less diverse and have more ancestry that's been in Britain for a longer period compared with urban areas which have a higher population of migrants."

"Some groups are reproducing at higher or lower rates. Populations in Africa, for example, are rapidly expanding, so those genes increase at a higher frequency on a global population level. Areas of light skin color are reproducing at lower rates." Therefore, Hodgson predicts, skin color from a global perspective will get darker.

"It's almost certainly the case that dark skin color is increasing in frequency on a global scale relative to light skin color", he said. "I'd expect that the average person several generations out from now will have darker skin color than they do now."

"And what about space? If humans do end up colonizing Mars, what would we evolve to look like? With lower gravity, the muscles of our bodies could change structure. Perhaps we will have longer arms and legs. In a colder, Ice-Age type climate, could we even become even chubbier, with insulating body hair, like our Neanderthal relatives?"

"Well, we really don't know, but certainly, human genetic variation is increasing. Worldwide there are roughly two new mutations for every one of the 3.5 billion base pairs in the human genome every year, says Hodgson. Which is pretty amazing - and makes it unlikely we will look the same in a million years."

Hmmm… that of course relies in part on us being somewhere in a million years. But on a more practical basis there are tools to enhance the human which we may need- to face for our more immediate future as we deal with the rapid changes in earth and our movement into the cosmos.

15._ So, here is more on human enhancement (from Wikipedia, enhanced by Lucy Jones).

"Human enhancement (HE) can be described as the natural, artificial, or technological alteration of the human body in order to enhance physical or mental capabilities."

"Three forms of human enhancement currently exist: reproductive, physical, and mental."

"Reproductive enhancements include the selection of embryos by preimplantation, genetic diagnosis, cytoplasmic transfer, and in vitro-generated gametes."

"Physical enhancements include various cosmetics (plastic surgery & orthodontics), Drug-induced (doping & performance-enhancing drugs), functional (prosthetics & powered exoskeletons), Medical (implants (e.g. pacemaker) & (organ replacements e.g. bionic lenses)), and strength training (weights e.g. barbells) & (dietary supplement)."

"Examples of mental enhancements are nootropics, neuro-stimulation, and supplements that improve mental functions. Computers, mobile phones, and the Internet can also be used to enhance cognitive efficiency. The notable efforts in human augmentation are driven by the interconnected Internet of Things (IoT) devices, including wearable electronics (e.g., augmented reality glasses, smart watches, smart textile), personal drones, on-body, and in-body nanonetworks."

"Emerging technologies: Many forms of human enhancing technologies are either on the way or are currently being evaluated and trialed. A few of these emerging technologies include human genetic engineering (i. e. gene therapy), neurotechnology (i.e. neural-implants and brain–computer interfaces), and cyberware. Also included are the various strategies for Engineered-Negligible-Senescence, as well as nanomedicine, and 3D bioprinting."

"Speculative technologies: A few hypothetical human enhancement technologies are under speculation, such as: Mind uploading, Exocortex, and endogenous artificial nutrition. Mind uploading is the hypothetical process of 'transferring'/'uploading' or copying a conscious mind from a brain to a non-biological substrate by scanning and mapping a biological brain in detail and copying its state into a computer system or another computational device. Exocortex can be defined as a theoretical artificial external information processing system that would augment a brain's biological high-level cognitive processes. Endogenous artificial nutrition can be similar to having a radioisotope generator that resynthesizes glucose (that is similar to photosynthesis), amino acids and vitamins from their degradation products, theoretically availing for weeks without food if necessary."

"Nootropics: There are many substances that are purported to have promise in augmenting human cognition by various means. These substances are called nootropics and can potentially benefit individuals with cognitive decline and many disorders but may also be capable of yielding results in cognitively healthy persons. Some examples of these include Huperzine A, Phosphatidylserine, Bacopa monnieri, Gotu Kola, Acetyl-L-carnitine, Uridine monophosphate, L-theanine, Rhodiola rosea, and Pycnogenol which are all forms of dietary supplement. There are also nootropic drugs such as the common racetams Piracetam and Noopept (Omberacetam) along with the neuroprotective Semax, and N-Acetyl Semax. There are also nootropics related to naturally occurring substances but that are either modified in a lab or are analogs such as Vinpocetine and Sulbutiamine. Additionally, some substances can be inhaled for a potential nootropic benefit such as Rosemary essential oil which shows potential for aiding memory and affecting mood."

"Ethics: Much debate surrounds the topic of human enhancement and the means used to achieve one's enhancement goals. An ethical agenda of human enhancement can depend on many factors such as religious affiliation, age, gender, ethnicity, a culture of origin, and nationality."

"In some circles the expression 'human enhancement' is roughly synonymous with human genetic engineering, but most often it is referred to as the general application of the convergence of nanotechnology, biotechnology, information technology and cognitive science (NBIC) to improve human performance."

"Since the 1990s, several academics (such as some fellows of the Institute for Ethics and Emerging Technologies have risen to become advocates of the case for human enhancement while other academics (such as the members of President Bush's Council on Bioethics have become outspoken critics."

"Advocacy of the case for human enhancement is increasingly becoming synonymous with 'transhumanism', that is a controversial ideology and movement which has emerged to support the recognition and protection of the right of citizens to either maintain or modify their own minds and bodies; so as to guarantee them the freedom of choice and informed consent of using human enhancement technologies on themselves and their children. Their common understanding of the world can be seen from a physicist perspective rather than a biological perspective. Based on the idea of technological singularity, human enhancement is merging with technological innovation that will advance post humanism."

"There is a neuromarketing consultant Zack Lynch who argues 'that neuro technologies will have a more immediate effect on society than gene therapy and will face less resistance as a pathway of radical human enhancement.' He also argues that the terminology or concept of 'enablement' needs to be added to the debate over 'therapy' versus 'enhancement'."

"Although many proposals of human enhancement rely on fringe science, the very notion and prospect of human enhancement has sparked public controversy. The main question to the ethical debate on human enhancement mainly involves whether there should be no restriction, some restrictions, or a full ban to the entire concept."

"To this Dale Carrico wrote that 'Human Enhancement' is a loaded term which has eugenic overtones because it may imply the improvement of human hereditary traits to attain a universally accepted norm of biological fitness (at the possible expense of human biodiversity and neurodiversity), and therefore can evoke negative reactions far beyond the specific meaning of the term."

"Michael Selgelid terms this as a phase of 'Neugenics' suggesting that gene enhancements occurring now have already revived the idea of eugenics in our society. Practices of prenatal diagnosis, selective abortion and in-vitro fertilization aims to improve human life allowing for parents to decide via genetic information if they want to continue or terminate the pregnancy. Even though these practices hold eugenic connotations, most are already deemed morally acceptable in today's society. 'Neugenics' deems to alter the focus of what eugenics was termed to be in society due to devastating historical events in order to understand that current advancements of enhancement are more of a benefit rather than a form of destruction from a moral perspective."

"However, the most common criticism of human enhancement is that it is or will often be practiced with a reckless and selfish short-term perspective that is ignorant of the long-term consequences on individuals and the rest of society, such as the fear that some enhancements will create unfair physical or mental advantages to those who can and will use them, or unequal access to such enhancements can and will further the gulf between the 'haves' and 'have-nots'."

"Futurist Ray Kurzweil has shown some concern that, within the century, humans may be required to merge with this technology in order to compete in the marketplace. Enhanced individuals have a better chance of being chosen for better opportunities in careers, entertainment, and resources. For example, life-extending technologies can increase the average individual life span affecting the distribution of pension throughout the society. Increasing lifespan will affect human population further dividing limited resources such as the food, energy, monetary resources, and habitat. Other critics of human enhancement fear that such capabilities would change, for the worse, the dynamic relations within a family. Given the choices of superior qualities, parents make their child as opposed to merely birthing it, and the newborn becomes a product of their will rather than a gift of nature to be loved unconditionally."

"Effects on identity. Human enhancement technologies can impact human identity by affecting one's self-conception. The argument does not necessarily come from the idea of improving the individual but rather changing who they are and becoming someone new. Altering an individual identity affects their personal story, development, and mental capabilities. The basis of this argument comes from two main points: the charge of inauthenticity and the charge of violating an individual's core characteristics. Gene therapy has the ability to alter one's mental capacity and through this argument has the ability to affect their narrative identity. An individual's core characteristics may include internal psychological style, their personality, general intelligence, necessity to sleep, normal aging, gender and being homo sapiens. Technologies threaten to alter the self fundamentally to the point where the result is a different person. For example, extreme changes in personality may affect the individual's relationships because others can no longer relate to the new person."

"The capability approach focuses on a normative framework that can be applied to how human enhancement technologies affects human capabilities. The ethics of this does not necessarily focus on the makeup of the individual but rather what it allows individuals to do in today's society. This approach was first termed by Amartya Sen, where he mainly focused on the objectives of the approach rather than the aim for those objectives which entail resources, technological processes, and economic arrangement. The central human capabilities include life, bodily health, bodily integrity, sense, emotions, practical reason, affiliation, other species, play, and control over one's environment. This normative framework recognizes that human capabilities are always changing, and technology has already played a part in this."

Of course, there are moral and ethical hurdles to consider, in the enhancement strategies that were discussed above, and firm regulations must be set in

But a humanity that can set in a democracy with human sensitive regulations and law can provide the protected informed consent formality to prevent personal, unwanted changes by all persons alive when an "Enhancement" need becomes truly, and democratically recognized- evident. "

The point is that we can enhance ourselves to be more prepared to move with the changing of our environment and begin the initial stages of dealing with an expanding Universe within the multiple world Cosmos.

The problem is we are not behaving in a way that gives <u>time to achieve</u> those changes.

CHAPTER 6: RESISTING WITHIN

The Way We are Now

Why do we act the way we do? There is of course the good, but is so often neutralized by (really unneeded) selfish motives. Here following are important theories about our personalities-the driving force for our actions. That is the actions that in the end lead to resistance to stop and analyze what is needed for our long-term existence, our crossing over that terminal edge of the Final Boundary. It is noteworthy that these impressions arrive from Personality tests, which are described following summarized from various works appearing in Wikipedi.[1]

Evolutionary theory: Charles Darwin is the founder of the theory of the evolution of the species. The evolutionary approach to personality psychology is based on this theory. This theory examines how individual personality differences are based on natural selection. Through natural selection, organisms change over time through adaptation and selection. Traits are developed and certain genes come into expression based on an organism's environment and how these traits aid in an organism's survival and reproduction.

Polymorphisms such as gender and blood type are forms of diversity that evolve to benefit a species as a whole. The theory of evolution has wide-ranging implications for personality psychology. Personality viewed through the lens of evolutionary psychology places a great deal of emphasis on specific traits that are most likely to aid in survival and reproduction, such as conscientiousness, sociability, emotional stability, and dominance. The social aspects of personality can be seen through an evolutionary perspective. Specific character traits develop and are selected for because they play an important and complex role in the social hierarchy of organisms. Such characteristics of this social hierarchy include the sharing of important resources, family and mating interactions, and the harm or help organisms can bestow upon one another.

---

[1] From Wikipedia, the free encyclopedia on "Personality Psychology".

Theories of Personality

" Drive theories: In the 1930s, John Dollard and Neal Elgar Miller met at Yale University, and began an attempt to integrate drive into a theory of personality, basing themselves on the work of Clark Hull. They began with the premise that personality could be equated with the habitual responses exhibited by an individual—their habits. From there, they determined that these habitual responses were built on secondary or acquired drives.

Secondary drives are internal needs directing the behavior of an individual that results from learning. Acquired drives are learned, by and large in the manner described by classical conditioning. When we are in a certain environment and experience a strong response to a stimulus, we internalize cues from the said environment. When we find ourselves in an environment with similar cues, we begin to act in anticipation of a similar stimulus. Thus, we are likely to experience anxiety in an environment with cues similar to one where we have experienced pain or fear – such as the dentist's office.

Secondary drives are built on primary drives, which are biologically driven, and motivate us to act with no prior learning process – such as hunger, thirst, or the need for sexual activity. However, secondary drives are thought to represent more specific elaborations of primary drives, behind which the functions of the original primary drive continue to exist. Thus, the primary drives of fear and pain exist behind the acquired drive of anxiety. Secondary drives can be based on multiple primary drives and even in other secondary drives. This is said to give them strength and persistence. Examples include the need for money, which was conceptualized as arising from multiple primary drives such as the drive for food and warmth, as well as from secondary drives such as imitativeness (the drive to do as others do) and anxiety.

Secondary drives vary based on the social conditions under which they were learned–such as culture. Dollard and Miller used the example of food, stating that the primary drive of hunger manifested itself behind the learned secondary drive of an appetite for a specific type of food, which was dependent on the culture of the individual.

Secondary drives are also explicitly social, representing a manner in which we convey our primary drives to others. Indeed, many primary drives are actively repressed by society (such as the sexual drive). Dollard and Miller believed that the acquisition of secondary drives was essential to childhood development. As children develop, they learn not to act on their primary drives, such as hunger, but acquire secondary drives through reinforcement.

Friedman and Schustack describe an example of such developmental changes, stating that if an infant engaging in an active orientation towards others brings about the fulfillment of primary drives, such as being fed or having their diaper changed, they will develop a secondary drive to pursue similar interactions with others – perhaps leading to an individual being more gregarious. Dollard and Miller's belief in the importance of acquired drives led them to-in effect-reconceive Sigmund Freud's theory of psychosexual development. In short, they found themselves to agree with the timing Freud used but believed that these periods corresponded to the successful learning of certain secondary drives.

Dollard and Miller gave many examples of how secondary drives impact our habitual responses–and by extension our personalities, including anger, social conformity, imitativeness, or anxiety, to name a few. In the case of anxiety, Dollard and Miller note that people who generalize the situation in which they experience the anxiety drive will experience anxiety far more than they should. These people are often anxious all the time, and anxiety becomes part of their personality. This example shows how drive theory can have ties with other theories of personality—many of them look at the trait of neuroticism or emotional stability in people, which is strongly linked to anxiety.

Biopsychological theories: False-color representations of cerebrally fiber pathways affected in Phineas Gage's accident, (This per Van Horn et al.).

Biology plays a very important role in the development of personality. The study of the biological level in personality psychology focuses primarily on identifying the role of genetic determinants and how they mold individual personalities. Some of the earliest thinking about possible biological bases of personality grew out of the case of Phineas Gage. In an 1848 accident, a large iron rod was driven through Gage's head, and his personality apparently changed as a result, although a description of these psychological changes is usually exaggerated.

In general, patients with brain damage have been difficult to find and study. Nonetheless, researchers in the nineties began to use electroencephalography (EEG), positron emission tomography (PET), and more recently functional magnetic resonance imaging (fMRI), which is now the most widely used imaging technique to help localize personality traits in the brain. Although these and related efforts represent very young scientific efforts, there are some developing impressions.

Genetic basis of personality: Ever since the Human Genome Project allowed for a much more in depth understanding of genetics, there has been an ongoing controversy involving heritability, personality traits, and environmental vs. genetic influence on personality. The human genome is known to play a role in the development of personality.

Previously, genetic personality studies focused on specific genes correlating to specific personality traits. Today's view of the gene-personality relationship focuses primarily on the activation and expression of genes related to personality and forms part of what is referred to as behavioral genetics. Genes provide numerous options for varying cells to be expressed; however, the environment determines which of these are activated. Many studies have noted this relationship in varying ways in which our bodies can develop, but the interaction between genes and the shaping of our minds and personality is also relevant to this biological relationship.

DNA-environment interactions are important in the development of personality because this relationship determines what part of the DNA code is actually made into proteins that will become part of an individual. While different choices are made available by the genome, in the end, the environment is the ultimate determinant of what becomes activated. Small changes in DNA in individuals are what lead to the uniqueness of every person as well as differences in looks, abilities, brain functioning, and all the factors that culminate to develop a cohesive personality.

Cattell and Eysenck have proposed that genetics have a strong influence on personality. A large part of the evidence collected linking genetics and the environment to personality has come from twin studies. This "twin method" compares levels of similarity in personality using genetically identical twins. One of the first twin studies measured 800 pairs of twins, studied numerous personality traits, and determined that identical twins are most similar in their general abilities. Personality similarities were found to be less related to self-concepts, goals, and interests.

Twin studies have also been important in the creation of the developing five factor personality model: neuroticism, extraversion, openness, agreeableness, and conscientiousness. Neuroticism and extraversion are the two most widely studied traits.

A person that may fall into the extravert category can display characteristics such as impulsiveness, sociability, and activeness. A person falling into the neuroticism category may be more likely to be moody, anxious, or irritable. Identical twins, however, have higher correlations in personality traits than fraternal twins. One study measuring genetic influence on twins in five different countries found that the correlations for identical twins were 50, while for fraternal they were about 20. So, it is suggested that heredity and environment interact to determine one's personality."

Unfortunately, the implant in DNA as a needed "Empathy Instinct" is at this writing not yet identified. (See, for example, "The Offspring" by D.M. Yourtee and L. R. Anderson-Newsom.) And finally, sub psychotic development aside, the real way we are now on a daily needed for basis and the promise of ways to change is only just of recent years been outlined by psychologists in a way that shows the possibility of adjusted outcomes for all of us.

One such is Personal Construct Psychology (PCP) a theory of personality developed by the American psychologist George Kelly in the 1950s. Kelly's fundamental view of personality was that people are like naïve scientists who see the world through a particular lens, based on their uniquely organized systems of construction, which they used to anticipate events.

But because people are naïve scientists, they sometimes employ systems for construing the world that are distorted by idiosyncratic experiences not applicable to their current social situation. A system of construction that chronically fails to characterize and/or predict events and is not appropriately revised to comprehend and predict one's changing social world is considered underlying psychopathology (or mental illness.)

From the theory, Kelly derived a psychotherapy approach and also a technique called 'The Repertory Grid Interview' that helped his patients to uncover their own "constructs" with minimal intervention or interpretation by the therapist. The repertory grid was later adapted for various uses within organizations, including decision-making and interpretation of other people's world-views!

That is, it is possible given the right background people that may move to more social behavior.

Humanistic theories: Humanistic psychology emphasizes that people have free will, and that this plays an active role in determining how they behave. Accordingly, humanistic psychology focuses on subjective experiences of persons, as opposed to forced, definitive factors that determine behavior.

Abraham Maslow and Carl Rogers were proponents of this view, which is based on the "Phenomenal Field" theory of Combs and Snygg (1949).

Rogers and Maslow were among a group of psychologists that worked together for a decade to produce the Journal of Humanistic Psychology. This journal was primarily focused on viewing individuals as a whole rather than focusing solely on separate traits and processes within the individual.

Robert W. White wrote the book "The Abnormal Personality" that became a standard text on abnormal psychology. He also investigated the human need to strive for positive goals like competence, and influence, to counterbalance the emphasis of Freud on the pathological elements of personality development.

Critical to the matter of "good outcome adjustability", Maslow spent much of his time studying what he called "self-actualizing persons", those who are "fulfilling themselves and doing the best they are capable of doing". Maslow believes all who are interested in growth move towards self-actualizing (growth, happiness, satisfaction) views. Many of these people demonstrate a trend in dimensions of their personalities. The characteristics of self-actualizers according to Maslow include the four key dimensions:

Awareness- maintaining constant enjoyment and awe of life. These individuals often experienced a "peak experience". He defined a peak experience as an "intensification of any experience to the degree there is a loss or transcendence of Self". That is, a peak experience is one in which an individual perceives an expansion of themselves and detects a unity and meaningfulness in life. Intense concentration on an activity one engages in, such as running a marathon, may invoke a peak experience.

Reality and problem centered–tending to be concerned with "problems" in surroundings.

Acceptance/Spontaneity–accepting surroundings and what cannot be changed.

Unhostile sense of humor/democratic–do not take kindly to joking about others, which can be viewed as offensive. They have friends of all backgrounds and religions and hold very close friendships.

Maslow and Rogers emphasized a view of the person as an active, creative, experiencing human being, who lives in the present and subjectively responds to current perceptions, relationships, and encounters. They disagree with the dark, pessimistic outlook of those in the Freudian psychoanalysis ranks, but rather view humanistic theories as positive and optimistic proposals which stress the tendency of the human personality toward growth and self-actualization.

This progressing self will remain the center of its constantly changing world; a world that will help mold the self but not necessarily confine it. Rather, the self has the opportunity for maturation based on its encounters with this world.

This understanding attempts to reduce the acceptance of hopeless redundancy. Humanistic therapy typically relies on the client for information about the past and its effect on the present, therefore, the client dictates the type of guidance the therapist may initiate. This allows for an individualized approach to therapy. Rogers found that patients differ in how they respond to other people.

Rogers tried to model a particular approach to therapy- he stressed the reflective or empathetic response. This response type takes the client's viewpoint and reflects back their feelings and the context for it. An example of a reflective response would be: "It seems you are feeling anxious about your upcoming marriage". This response type seeks to clarify the therapist's understanding while also encouraging the client to think more deeply and seek to understand the feelings they have expressed.

If one thinks about these last two personality descriptions, it is clear that the majority of people are capable of adjustment, given good and wise growth to adulthood, and the kinds of societal environment in which to make their minds up, as to what is their reference back to themselves. Humans facing the Terminus will need to be such well-adjusted persons!

CHAPTER 7: CRITICAL DECISIONS

On Passing Through the Edge

16._ The people in our world are now as Teilhard suggested an evolving new personality. Authors apology, however, it is not that benevolent personality but in a wider variety… a diseased one armed to obliterate its long-term future potential in wars, disregard of its earth and killing of those children who might have been the ones to save the rest.

We can look at this world population of humans with a face of reality. It can be argued that we have passed through the Edge and now are (already) approaching the Final Boundary- the Terminus.

How much time we have to sort ourselves out to be truly ready to deal with a life living into the cosmos is, of course, arguable. The environmentalists have said that the time to correct the damage to the environment was 2015, now past. A wide range of experts predict about 200-300 years are left to support us, without major calamities in starvation, petulance, and massive killing in greed for the little that remains to support life as we know it.

Even so, in the wide population, its "Soul", there could arise a great many Future Navigators… if children are intelligently raised… calm-mind free super creative people-who might enable the existing humans to be ready to move.

As said above. *"a humanity that can set in a democracy with human sensitive regulations and laws can provide the protected informed consent formality to prevent personal, unwanted changes by all persons alive when an 'Enhancement' need becomes truly, and democratically recognize."*

And as reported in Chapter 2 as to what got us this far- "It seems to be primarily these two attributes that carried our ancestors across the first gap, turning animal communication into an open-ended human language, memory into mental time travel, social cognition into a theory of mind, problem

71

solving into abstract reasoning, social traditions into cumulative culture, and <u>*empathy into morality.*</u>*"*

The point is that we can enhance many of us to be more prepared to move with the changing of our environment and begin the initial stages of dealing with an expanding Universe within the multiple world Cosmos.

<u>*However, that will not occur, unless within the huge mass of humans there is a growing core of people on board who have developed a mentality that honors in empathy all the others!*</u>

This chapter focuses on the way to create those persons now, without the need yet for physical or chemical enhancement of the human body.

Yes, now some people can live, heathy, contributive lives. But that argument won't work to address the future, because our movement into the stars is not possible now and we are on the verge of leaving millions in destitution.

And, if you want to stretch the point by arguing we could live on exoplanets, or earth analogs, this is way beyond practical possibility, as most are too small or if built as analogs, could not support even a small decimal percent of the 7.7 billion people now on earth. *In short, to move us into the Cosmos's Forever, we need time,* literally those hundreds of years before the Terminus.

Boundaries, think of it. There are so many of them, life is full of boundaries. Some are thin and quickly passed, some are thick, and it seems take forever to cross. Some are challenging so much so, and so tragic from poverty to starvation, or with help from caring to plenty and recovery.

Then there are some, where lack of courage and foresight, and careful planning extends their length to the edge of danger. That could be us. And there are far too many sunk in narcissistic behavior that is blind to the suffering of others.

In consequence, there is a most critical Edge facing the Final Boundary between a special empathy and the lack of it. *The boundary to cross is at minimum moral empathy, that says this consequence or that can harm my species! That is the one needed empathy-that must take hold when any one of us can be harmed.*

And it is this penultimate empathy, the one that must be heeded. It is lingering too far behind to challenge the darkness created by the too many humanity lethal challenges, from climate obliteration of our world to nuclear war, the final obliteration of humankind.

That boundary is either the last- the end of us or one that can be crossed given our recognition of an inherent human error. That is the failure of a universal empathy that challenges and overcomes imbedded-only personal needs.

The Omega Boundary

One wishes that there is good news. But simply wishing won't help! **The time we are in now faces the outer boundary of Omega, we have passed its first Edge!**

If we are honest with ourselves, we can view our current status clearly. Nuclear annihilation could occur at any time with the ongoing bellicosity among nations, and our earth is declining. In fact, the Alpha of our good fortune is past and we are every day approaching Omega. That can bring in the final gasp of breath for our human species, or if we awaken, an opening into an incredible management of the stars, the brightest forever we can imagine.

So how big is the boundary, how much time? Ruling out nuclear annihilation or the impact of a too huge asteroid, the boundary with our often-insane behavior could be far too few years away. The last years of these will be more challenging, with more human suffering than we can even imagine. This, wars aside, is because our earth is in the struggling stages of life. But, could we cross the final boundary still as human beings?

In central focus, humans now communicate worldwide and are an amalgam- a singular species. And we are now blending with technology to become imbedded in artificial intelligence. So, our world- wide interlinking communications could help.

We have met huge challenges so we can do this, move on past the likely termination of human existence, and change the structure, the ending of the Omega point, move our essence safely into the far future deep within the cosmos, but we must plan for it. And we must begin now!

Humanity has embedded in its psyche an ether of love, but it is being lost - evaporated in ignorant cruelty and inhumanity. That imbedded sense of love must be captured globally in the way we raise our children, and we must secure that with stable mechanisms in worldwide oversight. We must provide for our young a pathway that cements universal nationality and a sense of social responsibility. Then together we can work to conquer the stars.

Physical strength varies with time, aging, and as circumstances dictate. Moral strength need not be so vulnerable to the influence of time, it can be continually developed at every point in life, and it always matters most in the end! Human beings cannot make the journey across time when they are not imbued with the sense of total cooperation and sympathy for their species.

Starting now vistavien essence, true moral strength can become a part of us - the Sapiens.

It is developed first through recognizing and practicing a simple viewpoint appropriately called "Objective Humanism". That begins the process of creating a deeper understanding for youth development worldwide. The outcome will be healthy universally attuned persons who in their clear mentality know that they are a part of and thus care for all the rest of us.

The following defines this philosophy and after that are "Core Principles" to bring about the most mature upbringing of or children and those in the future.

Guidelines: Objective Humanism

<u>The Vistavien Pathway.</u> The future, protecting way is grounded on a special "Tactic of Behavior". This is the philosophy of people that work to secure the progress of Human Kind into the future! It is an enlightened mindset yielding a sense of personal strength and promise! The result is a protective blanket for children building future navigators who are armored mentally to create worldwide tolerance and peace.

Their way is in the practice of "Objective Humanism". It embraces at its core human reason and the freedom to practice it for all people. This means first its caring ethics! Then it asks one to reject dogmatic pseudoscience and superstitions as the main basis of morality and decision making.

This benevolent and wise philosophy is specifically a continually adapting search for truth centered by a sense of humaneness. It holds intentionally that people be mentally free so that they can guard reasoning against cruelly oriented objectives and anti-human subsequent actions!

Our ability to think, to be at first mindful and humane, is a gift so incredible that it would be the most terrible of all crimes ever-to lose that potential, through aberrations of greed and inhumanity.

It is a simple fact that we must - many more of us, see and feel it - our Vistavien Navigator self! Then, and only then, will there be earned for us - Heaven, Utopia, Shangri-La, Darul as-Salam, for all time.

That of course, is based upon enough time for us, the time to learn and grow, to practice our humanism! If we achieve that, the story of human kind does not need to end untidy as it happens too frequently now. Then it could actually be as it may seem from distant outer space, one world, One-people!

Following are practices to achieve widespread objective humanism and build in us the Vistavien Way.

SECURING VISTAVIAN EVOLUTION

We must think deeply about ways to elevate our humanitarian drive in order to approach that final boundary intact with those aspects of us that are our best.

To help in securing this there are two fundamental tactics. The first is guarding the way children are helped to be mentally free and self-actuating, so as adults they can make wise humanitarian-based decisions. The second tactic is in support of that forward one. This is oversight and response to that destructive infusion of cruelty and in-human morality feeding into the now existing worldwide internet — that is in effect, the "Global Brain".

 To achieve the second or oversight objective, it is essential for social and government groups to cosponsor "Strategic Webnet Armor (STA)". One such, as an example, entitled "SKIES" is given in the book "The Omega Shield" ISBN: 978-1-38-989564-7. These "Webnets" are centered with collaborating people united in purpose to circulate information countering that which harms the heathy mental growth of children.

Ideally, these STA will use the new world-wide computer network (on line forwarding) with information to help in developing healthy children at points where the influx of negative rubbish threatens the healthy maturing of children. Such groups are already beginning to form to disseminate information on damage to the environment and through organizations such as the child-heath directed publications by the World Health Organization (WHO). None-the less it will be critical for these activities to accelerate in numbers even in today's environment. Readers of this book may wish to help in this all-important information flow.

As said, the approach is twofold. The forward one is in the way children are helped to be mentally free and self-actuating so as adults they can make wise humanitarian-based decisions unhindered by anti-human dogma.

Within this approach is the clear thinking of Maslow, whose growth to self-actualization provides a fundamental wisdom for all people. This recognizes that the majority of humans have within an initial sense of morality, redemption, empathy, and broad humanitarian sensitivity. It is important for people to understand this growth pattern and the inherent requirements. *The protection of these critical senses and the natural growth toward becoming the magnificent creatures they must be conserved in the genetic development of each new generation!*

Underlying the preservation and optimal growth of these star reaching characteristics are three basic ideologies.

A. Protect Every Child
B. Secure Healthy Growth
C. Enable Freedom of the Mind

The following are descriptions of these ideals. They are available here for any persons or groups wishing to maintain the mental health of their children. Their world-wide distribution is one significant way to create path leaders i.e. "Future Navigators" for humankind into the distant future.

A. PROTECT EVERY CHILD

Irrational wars, starvation, faith-based crimes… greed against children threatens our future. Therefore, we adopt the following, a manifesto of values and behaviors. These following listed standards are to unite the highest doctrines of Humankind into a "Final Code of Conduct," the system by which our children will survive in peace, happiness, and productivity for all the future.

1. That there is no dogma in faith that demands converting, dominating, injuring, or killing a "non-believer".
2. That philosophical, political, or national dogma used as the reason for harming any person is deception amounting to crimes against Humankind.

3. That children will not be used as monetary capital for any reason. Capital means returning love to them.

4. That murder is an act of insanity; persons committing this crime will be isolated from the population.

5. That those religious beliefs based upon the values, characteristics, and behaviors best in and for all human beings should be harbored without prejudice.

6. That every child from the first dawning of cognitive ability should know that the whole of humanity is their family above all sects, states, or nations.

7. That every adult person will freely contribute every day an act to support planet Earth and an act contributing to the movement of the species throughout the Cosmos. From Earth's model, if needed, we will move all into and find ways to reside in the broader Cosmos, to create Earth like places, "Tera-Realms".

8. That all governments will be guided as their first principle by this; anyone in their population or within the government who denigrates, injures, or kills a child commits a crime against the species. Such species crimes will be punishable by isolation of the injuring party from the world population.

9. That every government shall codify these principles in the laws of their nation.

10. We vow to the upbringing and education of all children as enumerated following:

1.) Every child will be guarded and supported to the finest health and education from birth at every place on the planet. We recognize that any child could be the seed to the "Final, Perfect Ultimate Human." So, all will be given the chance to mature in a safe and supporting environment.

2.) We will begin all our actions by never removing hope from any child! We recognize the line between hunger, and anger is a thin line. Universal education of the world's children cannot occur in a world at war. We will work exhaustively to prevent the loss of young life through starvation or in wars of idealism. Complete removal of war will be the goal of each person on this planet.

3.) Each day, we will honor the following practices born in the faiths and philosophies over the history of Humankind.

Islam: From the faith of Islam, we adopt the following. Children have the right to be fed, clothed, and protected until they reach adulthood. They must have respect to enjoy love and affection from their parents. They have the right to be treated equally in relation to their siblings in terms of financial gifts. Parents will provide adequately for children in inheritance. Children have the right to education. A saying attributed to Muhammad relates: "A Father gives his child nothing better than a good education."

Christianity: From the Christian Faith, we adopt the following. Train a child to respect this idea: "He will do unto others as he would have done to him."

Judaism: From the Jewish Faith, we adopt and will hold the following. Girls will be given the same level and quality of education and the same in all rights as boys.

Buddhism: From the teachings of the Buddha, we will hold the following. We will support our children to become generous, compassionate, virtuous, responsible, skilled, and self-sufficient beings. We will give them the basic mental skills they need to find true happiness. To that, the most important thing is helping them to understand that every action has consequences. Each of those actions will determine their happiness, not only at the moment, but in the future. That is the basic lesson of karma, cause, and effect.

Hinduism: From Hindu belief, we consider the following. It is that one should discover and explore spirituality, religion, and God on one's own, and that we shouldn't interfere. It's okay to share and teach. It's another to misuse God to strike fear in others.

Pantheism: If you choose to believe in a god, hold that personally without evil intent to others. Recognize that each faith's prophet would have the main message from the same God; there would be no other choice, one believing in one God. In this there is thus-no reason for a polemic. However, above all rest in the beauty of the world into which you were born which is so sympathetic with your existence, in that alone is the unification of all faith.

Stand unified in those ideas, the same God, the same creations, your precious earth.

Atheism: From the Atheist, we pay attention to the following. Early implantation of religion should avoid damaging in the following ways because children are especially vulnerable to mental harms related to it. This includes extreme guilt about normal, healthy sexual functions, disrespect for science and reason, feeling war like toward others, which do not hold the same faith. Remember, free inquiry on all matters, strengthens the species.

Further to Protection of Children

We will help children along the path to self-control. This means they grasp reality, the karma of their lives. That means to understand things as they really are and to realize the truths of life, to see things through, to grasp the impermanent and imperfect nature of worldly objects and ideas. Since our view of the world forms our thoughts and our actions, this view, developing self-control, yields right thoughts and actions for all people.

Children will be guarded such that they grow into self-actuation. As that develops, we will open up for them education with a higher sense of purpose, the realization the Cosmos is for our species and provide an ideology that they are first Cosmos-lings! As they view this future, we will help them to understand that Earth is their glorious ark. It must last for thousands of generations. In its beauty, in the naturalness of earth's sympathy for our species, we have matured. An ideal it would be, that, even if most are elsewhere, this beautiful, so precious home would exist as it has been found until it dies, as it must, through Space-time forces against which there is no possible reversal.

Children will be informed as to the matter of how our species is improving. We have become aware that of all the species, our strongest suit is our ever-maturing brain. Our species agenda is to continue that remarkable development. This means that their Brain DNA in transferring and improving through the living generations insures the arrival of "Ultimate Humans". The young will be provided insight into this so that they may respect it as adults.

We will teach our children to join in the mission of feeding all the world population. If our Sapiens can mobilize to go to the moon, that same species can certainly mobilize the fair feeding of the world's children. The young should have full insight into this as the charge of all humans when adults!

Children will be informed about the conflicting forces that create behavior. The brain driven urge to destroy has been an embedded part of the survival of the fittest, yet that drive refers to the physical and with self-control can be managed. The brain driven urge of benevolence is also embedded. It is that drive that referees the preservation of the species. It is our strongest suit, the ability to think things through. The young should have full insight into this as a basic principle for reflection when adults.

Children will be allowed and guided by example into ethical and mental self-improvement. That is, resistance to the pull of desire, resistance to feelings of anger and aversion, and not to think or act cruel, violent, or aggressive, and to develop compassion. This education will avoid children into beliefs for which there is no substantiation.

We will teach the young that their children will be the next form of their species, the path to the future, and full enlightenment. This means that as adults, they will take responsibility for their reproduction. Wise and considerate human pairs will inevitably raise wiser ones. To aid children of each new generation adults will be provided an understanding of how natural development can lead in turn to their children becoming self-actuating naturally transcending. This includes where female and male interaction is equal without female victimization by men.

B. SECURE HEALTHY GROWTH

The buffer and the guide to develop healthy-minded humans in each generation is to respect that they have a psychology of needs!

81

Respect for this development in the face of damaging cyberspace, proselytization, and political influences will produce a more secure, self-actuation persons. STA groups come address ensuring that these are published to be recognized and fortified.

The human mind is complex and different motivations can occur variously in different lifetimes. They can be arrayed, however, much as in a pyramid, although each person from their starter knowledge may experience these differently, some in sequence others some aspects may occur simultaneously. None-the-less the fundamental transition in growth to an adult- to be respected is as follows.

Physiological needs
Physiological needs are the physical requirements for human survival. Although some will feel it redundant to relay the following, the world record requires this statement. If these requirements are not met, the human body cannot function properly and will ultimately fail. Physiological needs are crucially important; they should be met first. Air, water, and food are metabolic requirements for survival in all animals, including humans. And, of course, clothing and shelter provide necessary protection from the elements.

*A prime agenda of programs like STA is to make aware when societies are being denied this fundamental due to cyberspace interference in needed relevant communica*tion.

Safety needs
　　Once a person's physiological needs are satisfied, their safety needs take precedence and can dominate behavior. In the absence of physical safety due to war, natural disaster, family violence, childhood abuse---people may re-experience post-traumatic stress disorder or transgenerational trauma. Although this seems obvious, too frequently it is not a pressing adult agenda. However, adults have *a priori* responsibility to show children that they are concerned and making efforts to secure their safety. Achieving safety and

security needs include personal security, financial security, health and well-being, and a safety net against accidents and illness and their adverse impacts.

Love and belonging

After physiological and safety needs are fulfilled, the third level of human needs is interpersonal and involves feelings of belongingness. This need is especially strong in childhood, and it can override the need for safety as witnessed in children who cling to abusive parents. The deficiencies within this level due to hospitalism, neglect, shunning, ostracism, can adversely affect the individual's ability to form and maintain emotionally significant relationships in general, such as Friendships, Intimacy, and Family.

Humans need to feel a sense of belonging and acceptance among their social groups, regardless of whether these groups are large or small. For example, some large social groups may include clubs, coworkers, religious groups, professional organizations, and sports teams. Some examples of small social connections include family members, intimate partners, mentors, colleagues, and confidants.

Humans need to love and be loved by others. Many people become susceptible to loneliness, social anxiety, and clinical depression in the absence of this love or belonging element. This need for belonging may overcome physiological and security needs, depending on the strength of the peer pressure.

However, inherent in this is consideration of the social groupings that arise from cyberspace. Where that is obviously a dangerous influence, for example, suicide groups or terrorist organizations benevolent internet organizations such as (STA) should provide warnings and options to bring individuals back to rational viewpoints.

Esteem

All humans have a need to feel respected; this includes the need to have self-esteem and self-respect. Esteem presents the typical human desire to be accepted and valued by others. People often engage in a profession or hobby to gain recognition. These activities give the person a sense of contribution or value. Low self-esteem or an inferiority complex may result from imbalances during this level in the hierarchy. People with low self-esteem often need respect from others; they may feel the need to seek fame or glory. However, fame or glory will not help the person to build their self-esteem until they accept who they are internally.

Psychological imbalances such as depression can hinder the person from obtaining a higher level of self-esteem or self-respect. Most people have a need for stable self-respect and self-esteem. The psychologist Maslow noted two versions of esteem needs: a "lower" version and a "higher" version.

The "lower" version of esteem is the need for respect from others. This may include a need for status, recognition, fame, prestige, and attention.

The "higher" version manifests itself as the need for self-respect. For example, a person may have a need for strength, competence, and mastery, self-confidence, independence, and freedom. This "higher" version takes precedence over the "lower" version because it relies on an inner competence established through experience. Deprivation of these needs could result in an inferiority complex, weakness, and helplessness.

Caution should be issued by programs like STA where the influx of cyber space enterprises tends to lower self-esteem, and conversely, applications into cyberspace that help persons to see their value are exercises well within such an agenda. Programs mimicking that agenda are badly needed.

Self-actualization

"What a person can be, they must be." This quotation forms the basis for self-actualization. It refers to what a person's full potential is and the realization of that potential. *It is expressed as the desire to accomplish everything that one can, to become the most that one can be, and to become a good human being.*

It has the potential to develop in individuals who have been cared for as described above. Individuals may perceive or focus on this need very specifically. For example, one individual may have a strong desire to become an ideal parent. In another, the desire may be expressed athletically. For others, it may be expressed in paintings, pictures or inventions.

Protection of that capability against degradation of it from aberrant self-depreciating, addicting influences is clearly a priority of STA organizations.

Self-transcendence

The above life stages and needs were set down originally by A. H Maslow, who wrote on "The Hierarchy of Needs".

Maslow explored a further dimension of needs. *The self only finds its actualization in giving itself to some higher goal outside oneself, in spirituality or altruism, helping others.*

This involves Transcendence, a state that is a critical agenda applying to the ever increasing and inserting "Global Brain".

Programs like STA in their overseer role, protection of this state is fundamental to the optimal advance of humans. "Transcendence refers to the very highest and most inclusive or holistic levels of human consciousness, behaving and relating, as ends rather than means, to oneself, to significant others, to human beings in general, to other species, to nature, and to the cosmos."

If healthy, and the path can be supported, growing children will be prepared at some point in their lives to "Self-Actualize", and from there to explore the minds-eye, seeking stability and independence of thought. (to develop freedom of mind).

Children in that state express empathy! Thus released, they are easily recognized, and are set to interpret the way to reach their own goals at first on their own, and in that contribute to societies, benevolent and strong growth.

Programs like STA are needed. They will serve as one means to protect this growth potential, and through this create an opportunity for people to develop clear headedness, in open and capable analytic minds. The path to that (protected by such programs) is one of insurance and is enumerated following.

C. FREEDOM OF MIND

Insure Open Mindedness

Open mindedness is essential to maintain the sense of humanity that will derive from child protective and growth development programs. Via this means the protected, mature individual will resist the aberrant influences in cyberspace and other intrusions in rational thinking. From parent to a child over generations, the idealized will bring humankind into a star reaching Nirvana.

Here are steps, an education in *mind development* to be offered for all entering our changing world. This is a "Means Journey". It is a needed method requiring diligence to master, but well worth the trip.

1. Understand Chaos. We live with a sense of Chaos, but if it comes to ordering, if mental calm occurs, patterns can become aware and can be employed to move creativity. New thoughts are generated. We can gain clearer light. The following helps in removing the sense of chaos.

2. Know Dream Reality from Possible Reality. There is an edge to reality. We are often unable to grasp it clearly. It is as if truth exists over a razor's edge. Thus, we live in the dream of immortality. Be calm, realize it, there is the reverse side to everything and know that even the reverse has a reverse-ones we may never be able to see. So, then you are back to the only possible reality for you day to day, the present you! *Your Mind -- it is that which governs your reality!*

3. Respect the Cosmos. Remember, the Cosmos and our world are older than us. We are the end of a long chain of response. Whatever we do the Cosmos has a head start! Reality proceeds, yet the direction we (you) set may be a

part of that! If you try and try again and fail, the Cosmos is speaking to you. If you feel success, you are in the possible process!

4. <u>When Thinking do Work to Gain Freedom.</u> Freedom and security are interdependent, yet by separating them in our minds we grow. Security has a definite small connotation. Freedom has a large and unlimited connotation. Behind Security, there are sometimes artificial limits, when we are able to cut through them there is freedom. Freedom from those kinds of limits puts one within an understanding of how their lives really fit within the Cosmos. The mind cannot expand unless the center is preserved from artificiality. That is achieved by selecting wise limits with incomplete or arbitrary limits, the whole structure endangers collapse. A wise center allows for delightful freedom. (Protecting the center of one's mind; makes it a capable mind, then the future has potential to be protected.)

5. <u>Protect Your Mind.</u> The preciousness of your mind is impossible to underestimate. Use it or be abused by it!

6. <u>Make a Capable mind.</u> The cause is given meaning by noting the effect carefully! Know then that a single event is a tunnel through which all the events reflect. These two—cause-effect---cannot be separated. So, you learn to understand them, first in the minuscule which leads one to understand that there is the macro that is the most important. In bees, it is the multifaceted eye... *in humans it is your capable mind that can see that you see!*

7. <u>Overcome Interrupted Mind.</u> The mind is full of noise, contributing to that sense of Chaos. Focus until it quiets to a single sound! Then will occur but one voice. Silence, frees one from interfering internal dialog! (Some may prefer meditating to achieve this.)

8. <u>Overcome Troubled Mind.</u> Some have developed a library in their head that becomes but one book, in their view the "Truth Book." This only one book mind attempts to avoid becoming contaminated by outside ideas. This is a system with such strong limits that it leads to defending self, then to bigotry and wars!

9. Realize the Difference Between Belief and Freedom. Belief takes meaning into formalization, then eventually fossilization. However, if understanding is allowed to shift, each moment can be a path to freedom.

10. Believe Just First in Everything. Sounds confusing? But, much of conflict between people is from colliding beliefs. So, practice trying to believe initially in everything! Yes, that sounds strange, but internally, in time, the parts will sort logically, leading to one giant idea, hence, no limits! This should free one from the desire to be always right (which most of us have). Great problems can be solved, sometimes by evaluating the wrong. *One should rather be happier in ideas that can be improved!*

11. Allow the Time to Grow. Focus on nature, it has much to say. Remember the message in the seeds. Your time will come and with it a time to grow!

12. Understand Difference Between Fear and Courage. Fear is controllable. In fact, if you think about it, we only fear what we "see" in the future. The rest is anticipation! In fear, we begin to imagine what we can't do, rather than what we can. Dwelling on what you can't do leads to fear, dwelling on what you can do leads to courage!

13. Know Change and Learning Are Interlocked. To learn is to change, to change is to learn. There is no learning without change! To remain unchanged is to remain forever without comprehension.

14. Understand Perception in Relation to Reality. We must accept that there are both perception and reality. In fact, more aptly put, more relevant to us as persons, human life is "Attending." We can't turn it off. It is always pointing at something… as long as we are feeling we "Attend". In that time, understand the reality versus the perception of it.

15. Recognize the Modes of Attention. Within our attending, there are four modes: External and Internal, Narrow, and Wide. We exist or see an existence in one or the other. *Learn to know the whole!* When looking down also look

up, expand the narrow to the wide and vice versa. Your choices at any time depend on the extent you see!

16. <u>Expand Attention to Its Twelve States.</u> Contract and magnify as you observe, use your attention! To add sparkle to the world practice alternate meditation, knowing each mode well at first. That is, recognize deeply that there are 12 states of attention: three senses; sight, hearing, touch and four modes; internal, external, wide, and narrow to achieve 3x4 states. In your mind gain, switch from external to internal using each. This will help your mind to become richer, more mature!

17. <u>Know the Basis of Behavior and Perception</u>. We don't disagree over what we perceive (usually). We often disagree over what those perceptions mean to us individually! Thus, the behavior may be the person, and how we respond gives the behavior meaning. The response is a secondary feeling, an emotion! The original perception is the primary or internal feeling. *To free yourself from bias, change variously your sense of the perception.*

18. <u>Balance Change and Response.</u> Responding to the messages of change can create meanings, thus giving you choices, access to different worlds. Changing response lets one see the world as the opportunity! This is what we call an "Open Mind".

19. <u>Enhance Attentions.</u> Practice each so it grows, make perceptions big enough to evaluate, then the distance will lend to improved attention, enhancement, and greater value. In effect, become a "Mind Tracer."

20. <u>Learn Translation.</u> Learn to "translate" each state. Make light have a feeling, rock have fragrance. Intelligence is limited by the number of states one cannot master in this way. The more this can be achieved, the richer the life experience. This helps to join one in existence within the Cosmos. In unhappy situations, one shifts attention through this means to relieve pain or boredom.

21. Move External to Internal. A skilled Mind Tracer shift's attention, external to internal to achieve their skill. They see an external and envision its meaning internally. This means appreciating the mental processes of which there are two; "Defining" and "Exploring." Too much defining leads to narrow judgment and views, but it can be useful if balanced as it may lead to a more fruitful exploration. If one starts out with the basis of looking for something, they may find something even more interesting. Pioneering something in this way for a group means the pioneer may gain a very special freedom, a special feeling of accomplishment!

22. Know Type of Questioning Relates to Happiness. The essence of the human is to understand, to be attentive. So, the way in which questions are asked is important. When we question, we should use the 12 states to enjoy this to wander this to let the ordinary become extraordinary. Even so, the words used are quite important. "Why" is a question of dogma, leading two more Why's? "Why" questions, sometimes work, but don't necessarily lead to information particularly useful, because this is thinking virtually, totally about meaning. "How" questions are those with a more often useful basis. One is thinking about actions. "How" leads us to use our senses probing into time, space, and weight. We see the Cosmos as phenomena, take advantage of the universe's action on itself to accomplish! Our essence, our mind turns wishes into use. We are excited about this skill. The skill at this is the measure of your life. It's very much about "How"! (Example, now that we know the why, the reason, the best is not how do we proceed?)

23. Grasp the Importance of Context in Thinking. "Content," "Reality, " and "Timing" only have meaning within the "Context" that they belong. They are subordinate to Context. Therefore, our ideas about them are changeable. That is, these should be viewed within their specific diversity to allow one to arrive at an accurate understanding of them. We should want first to understand that process, even though in the end the outcomes become what are desired.

24. Understand the Basis of Feelings. Feelings prompt a "human fog." There are two parts. Primary feelings are those of warmth, pain, satisfaction, the actual world. Secondary thoughts are the emotions and responses, the

meanings we apply. They are how we think about the world. These can be and are most often mistaken, intermixed. Feelings mixing with emotions can lead one astray. We must evaluate whether information is appropriate between the two... knowing the difference leads to better decisions.

25. Calculate Connections. Dreaming or envisioning is not a place, but a process, a process of calculating connections between points. The insight comprehensively gained is in using the twelve states.

26. Recognize and Use Space in Mind. The mind has the property of space. Space is not just something to fill casually. In reality, within in it matter can be created from energy. Space can be thicker or thinner depending on how much has gone to matter. So, Mind space has tremendous energy and promise. *Mind when stretched to a new dimension is never the same; It is now accepting new matter (ideas recorded).* To accept something new one must "empty some mind space," then open the door and let the future in, endless possibilities can come from this.

27. Avoid Depression, Madness, and Lost States. This is when one has lost the RANGE of attention, i.e. the twelve states. They are not out of Mind but lost in a limited realm well within it. Perceptions are fixed! The mind is safest not locked in, but when one is exploring freely within it. To discover and reveal hidden inner richness is the most exhilarating work of all!

28. Realize Differences: Religion Vs. Science and Self. Although this is not to deflect from the happiness gained in faith, religion can deflect one's attention inward in a virtue versus failure appearance to God, i.e. one is to behave always in a certain way making them hostages in a sense. Science, of course, is humanities means to advance, but in addictive attention it can direct one's attention only outward. One becomes an aggressor for making change. In a sense, both fail to strengthen the individual as they abandon "Self-Regulation". One to be happy should first self regulates oneself, mind, body, and spirit. Once internally sound, one can then go out to see if that changes perception. Without self-regulation, peace can only happen in a perfect world

91

and must fail. Oscillate between the external ideas in relation to your foundation of internal strength!

29. <u>Know the Promise of Human Maturity.</u> "When one resides within a correctly dimensioned drum, the sound of a beating heart is greatly magnified. When one truly sees the magnificence of human possibility, the sound of future beating hearts amplifies one's own! Human kind has awesome potential, but only if it continues to exist."

30. <u>Seek Aging Well.</u> The body sends strong messages to the older. To respond with courage, recognize time is the one resource you have. Manage it well. Here, the most important thing is your own voice. Learn that even now what you say is heard. Complete-is each day doing! Incomplete-is unfolding! Blend these and the beauty of life unfolds. I am. Am I? Complete, Incomplete. With time ahead, you are incomplete!

31. <u>Guide Yourself Internally.</u> Wanting to be perfect begins with self-control internally. We think of the past as influencing what we should or should not do. Talking to yourself in the right way can ease the stresses produced by this. You have "Mind Police" built up in your raising and experience. These are what others want you to do, but you take control by your personal voice. Remember to change the "You" voice to the "I" voice. Internal You - leads you to some statement about yourself, usually hurtful. "I"- has a need to never tag negatively. With "I" you can change to the positive such as "I want to share my success". But do cease wanting to be perfect by the demands of the Mind Police referred to above. Give that up and stay with the best impression about yourself. That way, you avoid living in "a Police State." Relief can then be gained to refocus your future. Delight is felt when your own internal voice wins.

32. <u>Change Yourself Upward.</u> With each heartbeat, we are changing. Time is the master. All our "Life Waves" are sums of our simple waves, compiling (tangled rubber strings by simile, Item 43). So how do we best change ourselves, take control of the waves? Emphasize the "I" voice, drop the you "always will be". That is with the "I" voice you gain, in effect, you control

time. The "You" voice plants you in the past. Ignore it, emphasize the wonderful. The "I" voice directs you to your future. Mood is set by who is talking in your head. Be free of your past, the Mind Policing, it only continues to affect you.

33. Expand the Right "Mind Code." Pronouns (as above) are the way the Mind addresses itself. However, look at Mind as a verb. It is what the brain does! The brain's memory is in chaos and the brain itself is a combination lock for everything. These things can be brought up in several ways; one word will evoke several meanings. Being dumb is allowing just one door to open from the Chaos! Being smart allows multiple doors to open. Make a Mind Code for something important to you, anything stored or just hanging there, then bring it back and expand it. Once a bit of the Chaos is trapped (put in order) let it gather new thoughts!

34. Know Limits in Existence. Your life exists only in your mind! If your view of what the world is fixed, (such as what is the perfect religion, the perfect car, move) unhappiness is sure to follow. View the world as incomplete, with room to finish it. Knowing your Mind leads to knowing your body. This gives the marvel of reducing illnesses that limit you.

35. Know What Is Complete and What Not. For strong viewed people, the world is fixed, so every discussion is a fight or an attack. If thoughts are reopened to discussion, the world is open to many things. By knowing not to complete, minds are changeable. Each person can make this discovery, and a wonderful world is the result. Remember, "It depends is also changeable and depending." We search for new places when we have "transformed eyes."

36. Solve Problems and Issues. The approach to every problem, no matter how big or small can be mastered by an expansive process in your Minds-Eye. First take the problem and expand it to as large a field as you can, organizing it into a single picture in your Mind. Then rise above that picture to look down on it and *organize* the pieces. Now the clearer picture can be made smaller and lower it toward you. When small enough, insignificant actions are created, resulting in coordinated beauty and might! That is, the random

neural discharges of brain must be linked and combined before the magic of thought, and understanding appears!

37. <u>Apply Superior Meaning.</u> Wrongly, values and beliefs become the lens through which we look, and color the way we see the world. This turns the infinite into the finite! Rather, see the world as incomplete and possible. Practice finding several meanings to each situation. The "this and that" events should not yet have true meaning. First see without seeing "Meaning"; attempt to see what actually is! Once, the big pictures are manageable stay with that optimal, adjusting slightly as you go-as needed.

38. <u>See Together the World from Your Mind.</u> Nothing is completed in the world unless it is completed first in your mind. Once mastered, know what you can do and don't know what you can't do! There is no time when self-reliance wouldn't be an asset. But, seek people you can complement while avoiding those you are weaker with. At the beginning, these "Seeking's" may be muddy waters, but even muddy waters can quench a fire!

39. <u>Draw Opinions from Different Views.</u> The Mind operates differently among different peoples. Thus, the far northern people see the top and bottom of things (sun apparently rising and falling, only). The equatorial people see the left and right side of things (Sun apparently rotating east to west). Remember that while we see much the same (it is the same sun), there are differences in the WAY various minds see the world. Draw opinions from different views to gain your own strength!

40. <u>Recognize that You Can Change Ideas or Concepts.</u> Your Mind is extraordinarily powerful. One can use it to help oneself to change the feelings about almost anything, from pain to aberrant notions. There are two ways of remembering: 1.)"As it happened to you," and 2.) "As you see it happening removed from you." When it is "attached" you feel it right "Here"! When detached, you are at a distance from the pain or idea. If you run it backwards from that distance, you can find ways to control it until you get to the attached so that it can be rationally evaluated.

41 Change Limits into Perfections. The Mind can do anything through imagination; you can even envision greater imagination. In that state, you have the model! Knowing it well and with a method, what you can do is unlimited. Many institutions will not accept the unlimited. They think it is dangerous and set too limiting places in children. However, humans are born to fight over limits. The space in your mind can determine what the world will or should be like. It is born in you. One always wants to be right, sometimes making one confused. Remember, through with the newly activated space in your mind… more perfect things can be made out of air!

42. Seek the Unknown. Behind most everything there is the reverse, or the hidden, beyond your immediate vision. (Below the plant are the roots). It is also an energy that can be seen sometimes, worth the effort when one develops deep inner vision. It can give you power for an exceptional journey. Ask! Use your imagination that is the tie-in to the power. What you can compute may not seem achievable, but you know in your heart you can do it!

43. Understand Time Truths. Life can be compared to a rubber string, lengthening in time, along the way tangling, tangles representing trials, successes, and progeny making again more tangles. Then when fully taught the life string let's go, snapping, releasing energy, to return to the original state, and the energy is provided to one following. Matter will buy us, neither be created nor destroyed, only return to energy. This is the natural phenomena. You have thought control of the tangles, the balance that creates or destroys them. So, to do your best in life, recognize and balance destinations.

44. Be Wise in Destination Choices. The best lived lives see and understand destinations clearly. Choosing destinations involves two activities--1.) Comparing, 2.) Contrasting. These are 1.) What someone wants you to do, choosing it or me, as for example in religion, or 2) What you want to do. Comparing is using value differences, contrasting is using exact measurement, no value implied. In contrasting judgment is made considering things as parts, without meaning. Comparing is "the difference between it and me", contrasting is "the difference between it and It". If there is much emotion one is comparing, if not one is contrasting. As destinations are sought one asks,

what is the meaning in knowing this (compare), or what is the difference between these options (contrast)? One's delight is the measure of whether they are in proportion with these two, whether they are centered rationally within their Minds-Eye! That means also one strives for simplicity in life not determined by imitation of others.

45. <u>Find Your Center</u>. Analyzing "Space" filled with objects, the objects seem to become uneven, but there is a center to a flowing river, we can compute it but never really see it. One's Mind is full of limits, but there is a center. If one understands the ideas herein, one can find one's center. At the center is a surprise–a source of happiness, a sense of rest!

46. <u>Understand Feelings</u>. Each of us has primary and secondary feelings. Moods are secondary feelings, which are either attached or hanging detached. These feelings are similar to our two nervous systems, i.e., voluntary, involuntary. For example, we see a mountain. It is fixed, high with color, angles, and dark canyons. This is the "Content Code," the involuntary. It is there. The way we see it is voluntary. This is the "Mood Code." These two give our thoughts "Meaning." If we are afraid of height, we may see an ominous, fearful structure. If we have a different Mood Code, we may see the beautiful purple in the evening light on the mountains. That is, the Mood Code can be different from ominous, it can be changed so can the memory of things.

47. <u>Understand Precisely How to Use "Meaning."</u> From feelings, we develop "meanings" to events and things. All meanings are arbitrary, one's interpretation. The meaning of anything is the way we represent it in our minds. Meaning has the power to connect Mind and Body. For example, emotions (meanings) can be registered and affect our bodies. If one changes the meaning ascribed (example, it's a lousy world), that will change how one feels. Changing another's meaning could change the world!

Meanings are guided by the constraints of our history, often making things difficult. However, if we change the meaning toward the obvious in front of us (finding order out of chaos) all else can be automatic. The obvious is the law, for which there are real consequences (what you do now can affect what happens to you in the future). If using "You" the "and" says you are damaged, then you are a different person, a damaged one. Conversely, if "I" is used, you can change your perception of yourself and become un-damaged. If one connects the two halves of the brain (the obvious to the consequences) there is enjoyment in understanding direction, a sense of delight happens!

48. Recognize the *Flavor* of reality. Although we have mood and content codes, we may have different moods, depending on what content we see or know. So, we can change the character of reality, how we feel in relation to it in spite of the cosmic cause and effect. This is because the World itself has no meaning without thought we give it that through the state of our Mood Code.

Part of how we see reality is entwined with "Anticipation." If we anticipate a loss, then we are in a state of anxiety. If we anticipate a gain, we are in a state of excitement. However, knowing that moods are coded it is difficult to complain. One needs to imagine how they would code to feel in an "Up Mood."

This is not to say the world is just "Made Up." Because we have limits, we can't argue the reality per se, but we can adjust our thoughts to the "Flavor or Reality," that we choose to live with. One's life can be sour or sweet. It is a decision each can make in spite of the fixed cosmic cause and effect, within one's mind, through how they reflect on the world - change in their life can occur.

People and institutions set themselves up to define the "Flavor of Life" and expect you to agree that is the way the world is. However, there is never a totally correct answer you can live in a world you believe is right. Although there are Cause and Effect *"How" you deal with it is your choice!*

49. Become a Decider. In every journey one hopes to reach toward the end. The discourse you studied was indeed quite a journey but now approaches

that-concluding point. The last presentation concerns the question of becoming a Navigator, one helping others!

More than doer's maturity leads one to become a decider, making the Mind aligned and clear as outlined, then doing becomes automatic and we and the World are acting together. The mysterious is more knowable through the obvious, and we gain control of our minds. On the other hand, the aimless path consumes.

50. Navigating Others into the Future. Minds gained through the "journey" just taken can heal oneself and indeed, the world. Some last valuable recognitions, signposts with clear lettering, help toward cementing that goal.

What is needed so that one can (internal skills gained) externalize to be of value to others---the human species?

 It first is important, that each person heals self, and then they can address healing the world, as our humanity is built in, an inherent instinct!

The following thoughts center upon that possibility. They are as follows.
 A. Controlling the Structure of our Memory (how the past affects each one of us), B. Controlling Time, C. Understanding the Intersection of Imagination versus Reality, D. Asking Fruitful Questions about Your Life, and a most important thought, which is specifically *E.) Discovering that a Mature Mind makes you a Navigator!*

A.) Controlling the structure of memory. On the way to a healthy mind, one wishes to forget a "bad and frightening" experience, and certainly space for wisdom is needed in our often too crowded minds. Some of the past, of course, amounts to lessons of progress and is retained in respect. Forgetting the unacceptable, the wrong, the cruel, the selfish, though takes effort, but we have a direct control over how it affects us, because as we have learned we have control over the structure of memory.

So, being enlightened, we know, for example, fear can now be seen as arbitrary-an internal event, the internal component can be controlled. Fixed, Mind Books, can be re-written.

Control over memory means developing a simple set of priorities. *These priorities tell us in a nutshell, that we first mind our own business*! We are capable of doing this when we are prepared to supervise our own instruction without the usual limits!

One only needs to set as priorities; self-determination, that is creating their own future, avoidance of trends -- that gives us guilt in the end, Integrity--- thus not regretting our actions, and control of the central core, --that is the "Foundation of Self," which is unrestricted by useless boundaries.

B. Controlling Time. Being attentive creatures, or ones desiring to lead, the "future" has a significant meaning and, in fact, offers pressure in our daily lives. "Future" might be described as the consequence of present circumstances, making it in a sense static or limited. That is, to us, there are only two ideas of time. These notions are "ongoing" and "finished " ,which seem to "leapfrog" forever. They proceed and direct all our actions in a limiting game. However, we have control by stepping back, and simply asking, "What is ongoing? What is finished? "We have the power to decide to turn these into "Now is Dynamic," "Then is Static."

The future is, consequently, opened up to more possibilities. We select successful past ideas and continue to explore. We use our available tools to regulate thought about time, recognizing that to know one thing is to open the potential to know a thousand, if not today, then tomorrow. Well-practiced ability expects success with developing ability.

C. Controlling the Intersection between Imagination and Reality. This comes about when one grasps meaningful meaning. In reality, the world will do in time what it wants. Give the world the chance it will resolve everything good or bad. One then recognizes that the World sits between one's own "to be" and "to do." Our lives are within i.e. between those "Spaces". In that is the important intersection, it is the one between imagination and reality! If you control first yourself, then you can control this environment. If one does not intersect, that is trying to control this, they may become impoverished.

This says in a seeming paradox, but in truth-one must first become self-centered in minding one's own business-controlling one's own internal environment to achieve a really healthy and mature state!

If that were achieved, for each of us, there would be no reasons for conquest, conflict, or greed. We would all be safe in independence from each other, but by the same token, available as a success for each other.

D. Working toward answers for the central questions about life. One last thought lingers before one rises up to the Navigator State.

Each of us has most important questions guiding one's life (yes you do … if you think about it, although it you may not yet have addressed it).

When one achieves rational answers, one becomes finally "Mentally Mature" if that answer yields happiness! The way in which this question is asked though, is almost as important as its content. Otherwise, your "Life's Questions" can go a long way to making you quite dissatisfied. If the answer somehow defines who you are or your present state of being, you are dug in and potentially sunk. For example, if you ask, "Will this last for me?" You are headed into a yes or no situation that cannot succeed. Nothing here on earth lasts forever!

Here are some thoughts that will clarify this all-important matter and put you on the way to happiness and maturity.

Eliminate yes or no answers!
(1.) Change the verb tense and the interrogative. For example, it is not "How will I obtain what I want, but how did I obtain what I wanted?" The latter then leads you to open your future from success.
(2.) When your question refers to yourself in relation to others, reverse it. For example, it is not "When will they like me, rather, when will I like them"?

(3.) Leave out the specific person and avoid leading the question with, "Why or Where", as these lead to the need for the extensive context development. (Remember "Why" takes one into a world of dogma, etc., and removes you from yourself.)

So, if the questions are done right, you will ask overall, "What in this situation loves me and them?" If the questions done this way work well for you, they will fill you with delight! They will direct you to the "Something" you are looking for. They will become a true map a self-correcting life map, and that will be work done without effort because work done in a pattern of joy is work without effort.

E. Discovering that a Mature Mind makes you a Navigator. Navigation takes courage, the self-confidence, the ability to imagine, and to remain fearless, control over the Mind's apparent limitations.

Those capable of rising to this level are "Advanced Immigrants on Planet Earth", in a sense they can be "Future Navigators" who avoid the errors accumulated from the past and work toward the future for all people, uninhibited with superstition and artificial priorities.

Among them, those immigrants on planet earth are the many who have given us the joys of life, the tools to make it work.

We will call them "Vistavien"; they are exceptionally capable navigators because they know themselves - in a healthy way!

Each of us through mind-free- loving attitudes can become that ideal *Vistavien-Future Navigators*.

This should include you, born into a gifted, remarkably capable species of which you are to become a critical part!

ACKNOWLEDGEMENTS

Sincere appreciation is extended to L.R. Anderson-Newsom for the detailed editorial review, always a great labor with works as this that contain challenging contents.

1.__The discussion on "The Omega Point" is from Wikipedia, the free encyclopedia. Complete referencing can be found there as under "Omega Point".

2.__Regarding the Omega Point cosmology. Arguments are / from the main article by Frank J. Tipler, "The Omega Point Cosmology".

3.__ "The Building Blocks of Life May Have Come from Outer Space" was from the following public media: https://public-media.si-cdn.com/filer/Phenom-Rocky-Start-631.jpg and the inside cover photo is a BBC earth.com picture.

4.__ "When Humans Became Human" was by John Noble Wilford, Feb. 26, 2002, New York Times-Times Machine.

5.__ Stanford archaeologist Dr. Richard G. Klein, "The Dawn of Creativity" written with Blake Edgar and in a publication by John Wiley."

6.__ "How Did Humans Figure Out That Sex Makes Babies?" was by J. Bryan Lowder, JAN 10, 2013, as an answer to one of the Explainer's 2012 runner-up "Questions of the Year".

7.__The "Explainer" is thanks Holly Dunsworth of the University of Rhode Island, Cynthia Eller of Montclair State University, Helen Fisher of Rutgers University, and Wenda Trevathan of New Mexico State University.

8.__ PRB's website, shows estimates of the number of people who have ever been born. Estimates were first made in 1995, with updates in 2002 and 2011, and 2017.

9.__ Comments and author notations from "When Humans Became Human" , John Noble Wilford, Feb. 26, 2002, New York Times-Times Machine.

10.__The discussion and inclusion of other scientist's contributions on Bonobos was from "Bonobos Join Chimps as the Closest Human Relatives" and was by Ann Gibbons Jun. 13, 2012.

11.__ Is Religion the Cause of Most Wars?... was from an on-line comment 04/10/2012 04:09 pm ET, as updated Jun 10, 2012. This book's author post-scripted the comment with

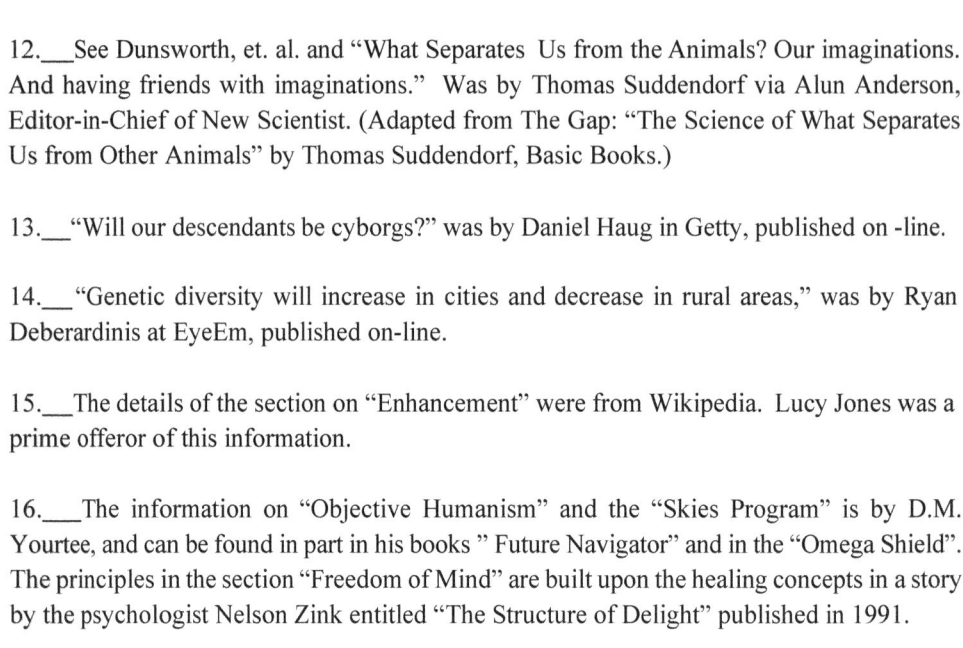

his own understanding from research in his book "Humanity and the Spirit Wars", ISBN: 978-0-615-72542-0.

12.___See Dunsworth, et. al. and "What Separates Us from the Animals? Our imaginations. And having friends with imaginations." Was by Thomas Suddendorf via Alun Anderson, Editor-in-Chief of New Scientist. (Adapted from The Gap: "The Science of What Separates Us from Other Animals" by Thomas Suddendorf, Basic Books.)

13.___"Will our descendants be cyborgs?" was by Daniel Haug in Getty, published on -line.

14.___"Genetic diversity will increase in cities and decrease in rural areas," was by Ryan Deberardinis at EyeEm, published on-line.

15.___The details of the section on "Enhancement" were from Wikipedia. Lucy Jones was a prime offeror of this information.

16.___The information on "Objective Humanism" and the "Skies Program" is by D.M. Yourtee, and can be found in part in his books " Future Navigator" and in the "Omega Shield". The principles in the section "Freedom of Mind" are built upon the healing concepts in a story by the psychologist Nelson Zink entitled "The Structure of Delight" published in 1991.

It was a wonderful experience to have available the thoughtful works included in this book. The authors and works cited show deep reflection on critical matters and reflect how remarkable we can be. Their comments have been transferred as intact as possible so as not to alter their intended thoughts-given the position and text flow needed to provide the overall account. Should corrections or omissions be needed, contact the author at Minds-Eye Manuscripts, LLC (Minds-Eye@bresnan.net). Those comments will be placed on the site http://www aminds-eyejourney.net and presented in the next edition of this book's essays.

ABOUT THE AUTHOR

This book gains its credit because of the thoughtful-perceptive by thinkers, authors whose thoughts   are incorporated.

It gains its argumentative character - to be blamed on the author, of this book, who has brought together thoughtful research and ideas in a challenge to all of you who have had the courage to read the works and stuck to that job.

That last-referred to-author is D.M. Yourtee.

Dr. Yourtee is Professor Emeritus, University of Missouri. To his credit he was lecturer in Medicine and Pharmacology for many years and accomplished humanitarian research as a Senior Fulbright Scholar.

He is, in addition, the author of books headed up as the "Future Navigator Series, Guiding Tomorrow" which was initiated through his book "The Final Human".[1,]

If you have made it through this book and studied the work, it is now up to you to be Author … a Future Navigator!

You have a sort of choice, to eat, drink and be merry, wasting away your life as too many do, or give serious thought to the future on behalf of the great grandchildren to come---to help them out of the tragic endings they are undoubtably facing in our rapidly changing world.

---

[1]Previews of these books at https://www. blurb.com>bookstore .
via site https://www.aminds-eyejourney.net/main-book-store

www.ingramcontent.com/pod-product-compliance
Lightning Source LLC
Chambersburg PA
CBHW051541120626
46551CB00013B/1325